METALLICA
BASS
Riff by Riff™
VOLUME 2

BY STEVEN HOFFMAN

Front cover credits:
Photo of Cliff Burton by Ross Halfin
Photo of Jason Newsted by Anton Corbijn
Photo of Robert Trujillo by Mark Leialoha

Title page photo by Michael Agel

Management by Q Prime Inc.

Music examples transcribed by Steve Gorenberg
Additional transcribing by Steven Hoffman

Cherry Lane Music
Educational Director/Project Supervisor: Susan Poliniak
Director of Publications: Mark Phillips
Manager of Publications: Rebecca Quigley

ISBN 1-57560-694-1

Visit our website at www.cherrylane.com

Table of Contents

Introduction

Metallica has earned themselves a spot in heavy metal's elite, joining the ranks of Black Sabbath, Ozzy (solo), Deep Purple, and Iron Maiden, among not too many others. They are without question the modern kings of metal. They have carved out a sound unlike anyone else's and spawned many bands who can only hope to reach their brilliance, artistic integrity, and stature. I remember the first time I heard Metallica back in 1985. It was Cliff Burton's amazing bass solo "(Anesthesia)—Pulling Teeth" from *Kill 'Em All*. My jaw nearly hit the floor. I was blown away that someone could make the bass sound that way and play with such ferociousness. After that, I made it my ambition to learn every song on every album that Metallica put out.

Their sound has always been the cutting edge for metal. 1983's *Kill 'Em All* introduced the world to the rhythmic precision of speed metal with songs like "Whiplash," "Hit the Lights," and "The Four Horsemen." *Ride the Lightning* refined the sound with more gnarly guitar tones, intense drumming, and thought-provoking lyrics. *Master of Puppets* perfected the speed metal sound—every track was a masterpiece in its own right, full of ultra-complex and driving rhythms. The release . . . *And Justice for All* took the music even a step further with lengthy magnum opuses such as " . . . And Justice for All," and "To Live Is to Die." The band also stepped into the video arena on this album, producing their first ever for the song "One."

But Metallica truly conquered the world with the release of *Metallica* (also known as the "Black Album"). This album had the perfect combination of their signature metal intensity with a new commercial sensibility. Every kid on the planet wanted to learn the riff to "Enter Sandman." Metallica commanded respect and was appreciated by a whole new generation of fans. Throughout the '90s, Metallica continued to put out albums such as *Load* and *Reload*, assuring their place at the top of the metal heap.

They also took chances. Since the early days, they were putting out singles of their favorite covers. From the first *Garage Days Revisited* released as a picture disc in 1984, to the *Garage Days Re-revisited* in 1987, to the *Garage Inc.* release in 1998, they abandoned the mega-production process of their official studio releases in favor of that "not very produced" rawness that the fans craved. And how about *S&M* with the prestigious San Francisco Symphony? Metallica's music suits itself quite well to a symphonic setting, and this album is a testament to how far reaching and influential their music is.

With their most recent release, *St. Anger*, Metallica still manages to turn heads and ears. Songs like "Frantic," "Some Kind of Monster," "Sweet Amber," "St. Anger," and the others all have elements of their classic tunes of yore: heavy guitar riffs, over-the-top drumming, and substantial lyrical content—all with a sound that rings strong with the present and future. Although void of a permanent bassist at production time, producer Bob Rock filled the bass boots on the album with authority, keeping the expert bassmanship tradition true to predecessors Cliff Burton and Jason Newsted. In 2003, Metallica added killer veteran bassist Robert Trujillo (Suicidal Tendencies, Infectious Grooves, Ozzy) to the lineup, and they now sound as strong as ever. (For a good look at them with this lineup, check out the DVD that accompanies the *St. Anger* album.)

This book is dedicated to exposing you to a chunk of the bass highlights from the Metallica repertoire in *Reload*, *Garage Inc.*, *S&M*, and the brand-new *St. Anger*, plus a selection from the *Mission: Impossible: 2* soundtrack. There is a good balance of theory and technique in each example, so you can learn how to play each riff and get an idea of what is going on musically as well. The vintage Metallica riffs have always been a challenge to play with precision, and many of the newer riffs are no exception. Take your time with the examples and enjoy the book. I know I enjoyed putting it together.

Rock on.

About the Author

Steven Hoffman has been a bassist for over 20 years, performing in styles that range from heavy metal to classical. Residing in Sonoma County, California, he currently plays upright bass in numerous Bay Area symphonies and opera companies. He also plays with Sweetleaf, a Black Sabbath/Ozzy tribute band (http://listen.to/sweetleaf/).

Steven Hoffman

Steve was an attendee of Berklee College of Music and received his B.A. in music composition from the University of California at Berkeley. He has been a private bass teacher for over 12 years, teaching a wide variety of techniques at Stanroy Music Company in Santa Rosa, CA.

Steven is trying desperately to get a website going. When he finally does (hopefully in our lifetimes), the web address will be
http://www.bassspace.com.

Acknowledgments

First and foremost, I want to thank my family—my wife Heidi, my kids Cody and Ella, and my parents—for dealing with me. Thanks to my teacher Karen Zimmerman for inspiration and showing me a higher level of performing. Thanks to my friend Steve Smyth for jamming with me over all the years. Thanks to everyone at Stanroy Music. And, finally, thanks to all of the students I currently teach and have taught over the years. I've learned as much from you as hopefully you have from me.

Gear Lists

Cliff Burton

Basses
Aria Pro II
Rickenbacker

Amps
Marshall
Mesa/Boogie
Randall

Jason Newsted

Basses
Sadowsky Four- and
Five-Strings
1958 Fender Precision
1981 Spector NS
. . . among *many* others

Amps
Ampeg SVT
SWR

Effects
Multiple Boss Pedal
Effects

Bob Rock

Basses
Vintage Spector

Amps
Vintage Ampeg SVT with
8x10 Cabs
Marshall SuperBass 100-
Watt Head
Tech 21 SansAmp

Effects
Dunlop Wah

Robert Trujillo

Basses
Tobias Five-String (Retired)
Music Man Stingray Five-
String
MTD Designs Five-String
Fernandes Five-String

Amps
Ampeg SVT II Heads
Ampeg 8x10 Pro Series Cabs
Mesa Boogie Dual Rectifier
Head
Mesa Boogie 4x12 Cabs

Effects
Morley Wah
Boss Chorus and Flange

RELOAD

Fuel

Words and Music by
James Hetfield, Lars Ulrich and Kirk Hammett

OPENING RIFF

For this song, tune down one half step to match the pitches of the recording. The opening riff comes at you with teeth like so many other Metallica riffs. Based on the E minor pentatonic scale, it uses rhythmic displacement to drive the G through the Es, before cadencing on the A5 chord. The pull-offs help to enhance the texture of the sound, while the accents on each G define the polyrhythm within the 4/4 groove.

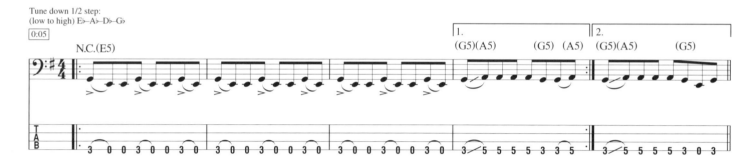

CRUISING RIGHT ALONG

Moving through the chord progression of the Verse, Newsted weaves a line that defines each chord as he plays melodically, taking advantage of the spaces between the vocal lines. In measures 1 and 2, he uses a descending E blues scale to respond strongly to Hetfield's vocal phrase. In the following measures, Newsted creates a motivic line over the chromatically moving chord progression. Working from the E blues scale, measures 4 and 5 are rhythmically and melodically identical, except that measure 5 is a half step lower to compensate for the B♭5 chord.

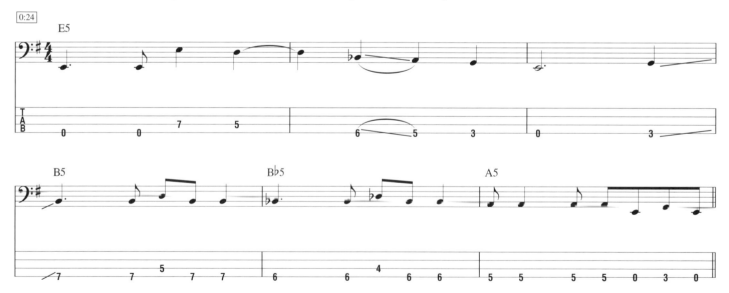

CHORUS RIFF

Throughout the Chorus, the bass line stands as a testament to playing simply and appropriately to stress the driving nature of the tune. As Hetfield sings about the churning of engines, Newsted's bass line does just that, chugging through with steady eighth notes, reinforcing the double bass drum beat and the chords at hand, and sticking in transitioning notes between each chord. These are things that every bass player should have in their arsenals.

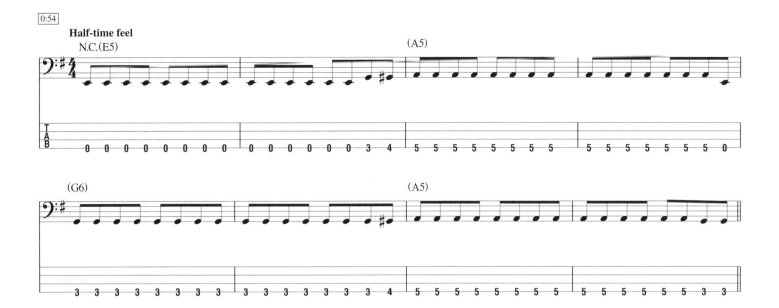

CHORUS VARIATION

At the final Chorus, Newsted expands upon his line to come up with a variation that borrows from both the Chorus and Verse. As he drives the chord, he makes use of a lower neighbor tone (B) to help propel the line to the D chord where an upper neighbor tone (E) is used. This is reminiscent of the opening riff's rhythmic structure.

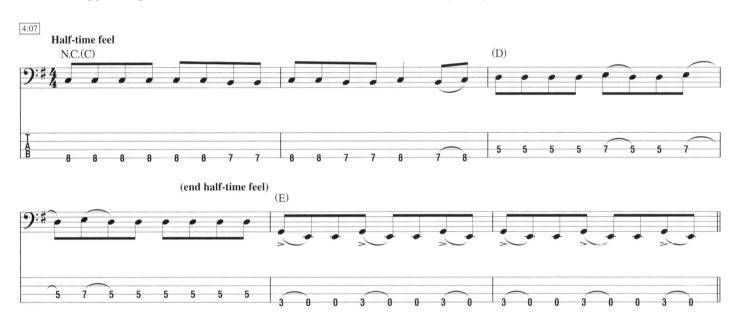

The Memory Remains

Words and Music by
James Hetfield and Lars Ulrich

OPENING GROOVE

For this song, tune down one half step if you want to match the pitches of the recording. The opening groove is a heavy, melodic jam using the E minor pentatonic scale. Each two-measure phrase starts out with bass and guitars doubling each other with octave Es. In the second measure, the bass breaks away from the guitar melody with a counter line that both supports the guitar line and speaks independently as well. While the guitar line goes up the blues scale, Newsted stays low on the E, sliding big off the low G to the upper octave of E and then to a D. It all ends with a big pentatonic riff, starting on the high E and moving down the upper half of the scale. Newsted touches on C♯, implying a more modal finish with the Dorian scale.

Tune down 1/2 step:
(low to high) E♭–A♭–D♭–G♭

CHORUS GROOVE

Newsted does a fine job of supporting the vocal line in the Chorus. He rhythmically accentuates each lyric at the beginning of each measure via the D to the E while holding solid on the low E. The quarter note octaves amidst the pulsing eighth notes on beat 3 help to give space to the line and accentuate the lyric that anticipates the beat. At the tag of the second ending of the Chorus (shown here), Newsted uses roots and 5ths to play through the F and G chords, first with quarter notes on the F chord and culminating with eighth notes on the G chord, before sliding down from the D.

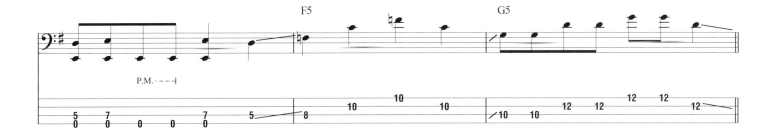

GUITAR SOLO SECTION

The guitar Solo section uses the Verse riff as its groove source. At measure 4, Newsted does a cool variation on the theme, playing double stops in 4ths with the root of the line taking the bottom voice. He sets up the accented D with a quick 16th note E minor pentatonic riff from the A before resuming with the solid low Es. At measures 8 and 9, Newsted again uses roots and 5ths under the F5 and G5 chords. He reverses what he did in the previous section, playing eighth notes on the F5 and quarter notes on the G5 to help catapult the line into the next section.

BRIDGE SECTION

During the eerie Bridge section, Newsted lays down a stable line that both defines each chord and supports the vocal line. Measure 1 gets busy with moving eighth note octave Es, before moving to the B5 chord with eighth notes as well. He sets up the G5 chord with a little turn, playing both the root of a B chord and the 3rd of a G. In the third measure, he uses the B to help steer the line to the D5, also using the C as a passing tone. In the last measure, he nails the root and 5th of each chord.

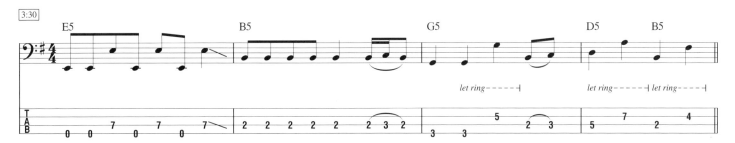

Words and Music by
James Hetfield and Lars Ulrich

Devil's Dance

FUZZED OUT

For this song, tune your bass down one whole step if you'd like to match the pitches of the recording. The opening riff of the song starts with solo bass playing a heavy, bluesy riff through distortion. The riff is based on the E blues scale, highlighted by the opening B♭ (the blue note of the scale) sliding down the neck to nail the open staccato Es. The line proceeds to "dance" above the E, bouncing around the 3rd and 4th of the scale before finishing with a turn-around riff using all those notes to take us back to the Es once again. This line acts as a cool counterpoint to the upcoming guitar riff.

Tune down 1 step:
(low to high) D–C–F

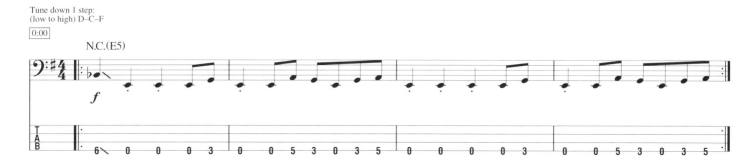

VERSE RIFF

The Verse riff shows Metallica in classic form, utilizing an array of rhythmic diversity to create a complex yet flowing line. The chunky use of eighth notes contrasts the guitar's rhythm, holding the groove solidly in place. Measure 4 has a bluesy whole step bend on the E string from the 5th fret A to B, before leading into the G. The rhythm at this point gets even more complex, with anticipated 16th notes between the first and second beats and mixed rhythms in the third and fourth beats.

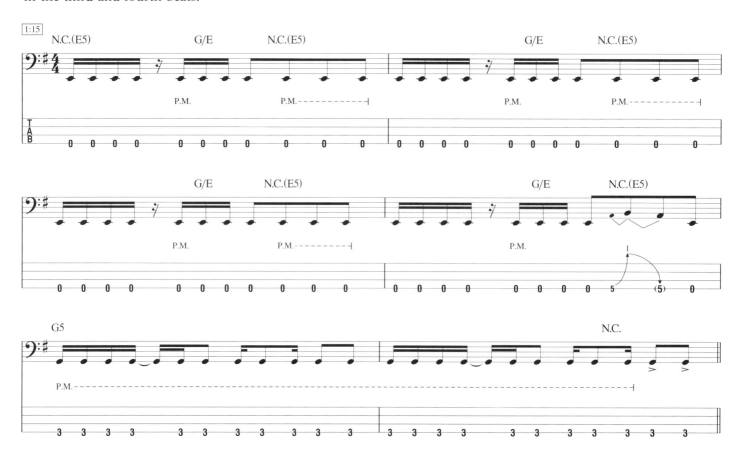

CHORUS RIFF

The Chorus riff starts on the ♭5 chord of E minor, using a stuttering rhythmic pattern of 16th and eighth notes. This pattern works best when you can feel the beat and be able to play around it, allowing the rhythm to dance. A B♭ grace note helps to propel the line downwards into the A and through the rest of the E blues scale. The riff finishes with a tradeoff between Es and Gs, recalling parts of the opening riff.

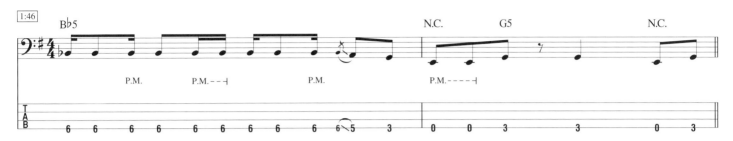

VERSE LICK

Late in the song, in the third Verse, Newsted pulls out an interesting bass lick. He first defines the F♯5 chord by playing the root and then the fifth (C♯). Going to beat 4 of the second measure, he slides to the minor 3rd of the chord (A) on the 7th fret and nails out octaves off the open string, sliding out and catching the B♭ to resume the main riff (not shown).

The Unforgiven II

Words and Music by
James Hetfield, Lars Ulrich and Kirk Hammett

VERSE RIFF

Tune down one half step if you'd like to match the pitches of the recording. The Verse consists of a chord progression based in the key of A minor; the bass line rolls through it effortlessly, naturally setting up each chord with passing tones. Newsted makes ample use of the scale: every note he uses is within A minor and helps to connect the chords to each other. Starting with the A minor chord, Newsted connects to the C major chord with a passing B. As the line moves on from the C, the G chord is set up with more passing tones (the B and the A), as the line now moves in the other direction. The G is a natural set-up for the E minor chord, as G is the 3rd of that chord; similarly, the E is a natural set-up for the A minor chord because the E is the 5th of that chord. Notice in measures 3 and 4 how the C chord goes to the high G via a major pentatonic lick in C.

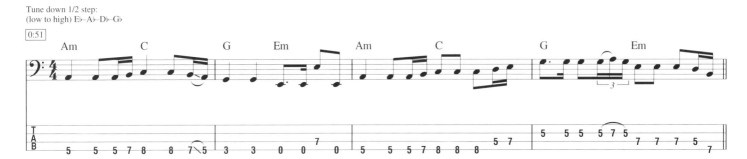

CHORUS RIFF

The Chorus riff is good example of how the bass can interact and support the vocal line. It consists of primarily 16th notes that are best played either with alternating fingers in your right hand or alternate picking ("down-and-up" picking) for consistency. Newsted anticipates certain chords by a 16th note to add strength to the vocals. In measure 1, on the last 16th note of beat 3, he goes to the B right on the lyric "known." In measure 2, he again uses a passing tone B, this time to connect to the A chords in the next measure. This type of 16th note anticipation happens again at the end in beat 3 of measure 4, going to the G chord. He then slides up the neck and finishes with a lick that supports the guitar line. Try to accent the anticipated notes to help feel the change of the chords.

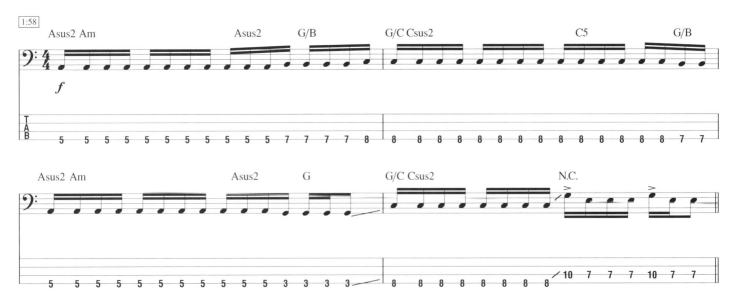

CHORUS ENDING

At the end of the first Chorus, Newsted does some fancy collaborating with the drums, playing variations on the groove. Measures 3 and 4 have him nailing 16th notes on the strong beats of the measure (1 and 3), shadowing the bass drum. In measure 4, Newsted also locks in the snare drum, mirroring its rhythm and throwing a smart lick at the end—he slides with his 3rd finger from the D to the E to help set up a good hand position for the line in the next Verse.

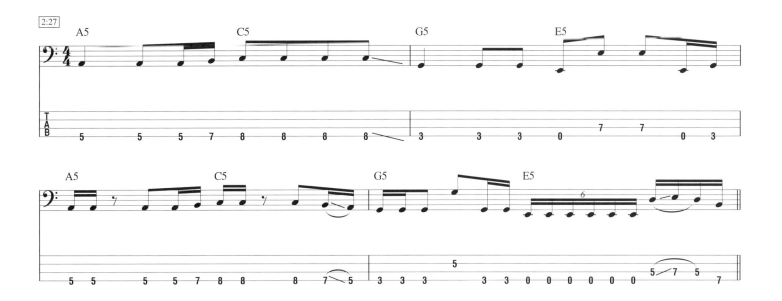

GUITAR SOLO SECTION

Here, Newsted is given the room to expand his line. In measure 1 of this example, he makes use of numerous techniques. His line is in a constant lock with the drums, nailing the pattern of the bass drum and supporting the snare. Slides are used at almost every chord change. Sometimes the slide is a way to play many passing tones in a short amount of space, such as in measure 2 with the G5 and E5 chords. It is also an effective way to move through long distances on the neck. The E octaves show a great example of this technique—the incorporation of the open string frees your hand to slide anywhere on the fingerboard. This use of octaves is an effective way to open up the sound of a line while maintaining the harmonic integrity of a chord. Newsted does this not only on the Es, but with the Gs as well for the culmination of the section.

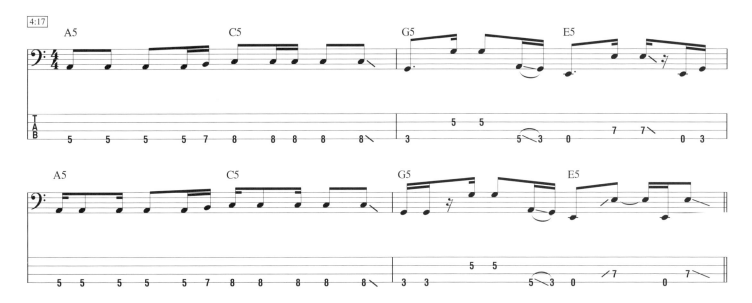

Words and Music by
James Hetfield and Lars Ulrich

Better Than You

OPENING RIFF

Tune your bass down one half step for this song if you'd like to match the pitches of the recording. This main riff finds its way into almost every section of the song, but the opening version is the most interesting. Newsted gives us a healthy dose of double stop playing in this section, doubling both the guitar part and holding steady on the low E. Keeping his fingers clear of the E string, he is able to play two notes at the same time on the A and E strings. Essentially, he uses the top voice to double the guitar part and eventually the vocals, with accents on several strong beats to ensure the timing. On the fourth ending, Newsted further reinforces the key of E minor with an E minor pentatonic lick.

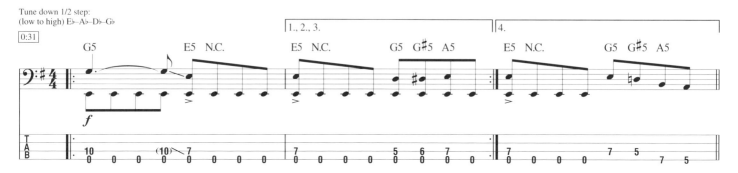

VERSE RIFF (PART 1)

The Verse riff is very straightforward but effective in its timing with the vocals. The line stays mainly on the root of the chords, locking in rhythmically with the vocal line and drums, before ending with the main riff.

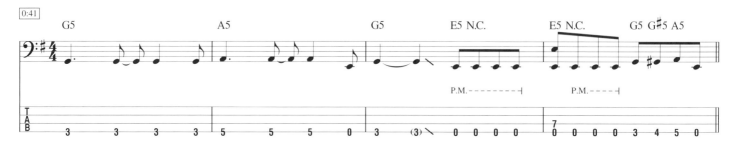

VERSE RIFF (PART 2)

Towards the end off the Verse, the groove picks up steam with running eighth notes, yet Newsted still manages to catch much of the rhythm of the vocal line.

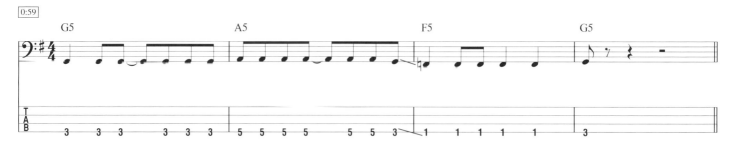

THE BRIDGE

Newsted does some nice fingerboard work at the end of this section, making great use of slides. In measure 2, he uses the sustain from his right-hand attack to carry his line through the measure, landing on an F before traveling a huge distance in an eighth note's time up the E string to the high G. Use your 1st finger from the low F to carry you all the way up the neck. Stay on the 1st finger so that when you slide back down to the low G, your positioning will be set up for the remainder of the riff.

CHORUS LICK

At the end of the last Chorus section, Newsted shows his knack for precision timing with this heavily accented lick utilizing octave Es. Accents are played by striking the string with more conviction than a normal attack, but not "over hitting" it. These notes simultaneously emulate the drum fills. Notice how only the octaves are accented, filling out his tone at crucial times.

Slither

Words and Music by
James Hetfield, Lars Ulrich and Kirk Hammett

VERSE RIFF

Tune down one half step for this song if you want to match the pitches of the recording. The Verse riff is based on the E blues scale. Played at the lower part of the fingerboard, the half step bend on the low G can be hard to manage unless you use two fingers—the 2nd and 3rd. This will give you enough strength to make the bend happen, while also setting up your hand positioning to grab the B♭ with your first finger. For total accuracy, practice by playing the note a half step up from G (G♯) and then try to match the pitch with the bend.

Tune down 1/2 step:
(low to high) E♭–A♭–D♭–G♭

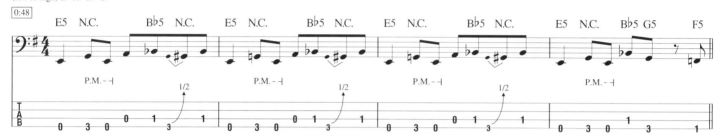

PRE-CHORUS RIFF

This riff is vintage Metallica and includes their "chunky" rhythmic style that creates a heavy vibe. The E and the F have a half step relationship to each other, and when coupled with the G, they give a darker color to the existing E minor key. There is some cool interaction between the instruments and the voice—as one calls, the other responds. The accent on the eighth note G at the end of the phrase heightens the rhythmic stress.

CHORUS RHYTHM

As the Chorus plays out, Newsted's rhythm gets more complex while he adds in some bluesy riffs. In the first measure of the example, Newsted lays down some chromatic passing tones—following the guitars—that help the G chords to flow into the C5. Once that C is established, his attention is towards the drums—he follows their bass sounds while once again throwing in bluesy passing tones to the A5. At the end of the riff, the offbeat accents help to propel the groove to its peak. Notice the muffled notes in the last measure. You can execute these by muting the E string either with your left hand on the string or, if you are using a pick, palm muting with your right hand as you strike the string.

CHROMATIC TURN

During the first section of the guitar Solo, Newsted plays a cool chromatic turnaround riff before heading back to the E. This lick will utilize all four of your left-hand fingers if you keep your first finger on the F# and let the others fall naturally on the other notes.

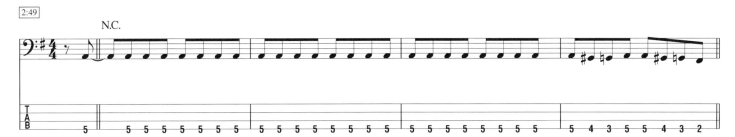

OUTRO RIFF

After the Outro guitar solo, the song heads back to the Chorus riff. At this point in the song, Newsted takes liberties with his line, adding double stops, muted notes, and slides. In measure 1, as his line moves down to the C5 chord, a C# is paired with an open E before falling to the B—the B is a great "setup note" for the C5. In measure 2, Newsted slides back up to the E and then employs a bluesy chromatic run to get to the A. Measure 3 utilizes the A minor pentatonic scale to solidify the A tonality. Notice the muted notes in measure 4; they give the groove some welcome chunkiness.

Carpe Diem Baby

Words and Music by
James Hetfield, Lars Ulrich and Kirk Hammett

INTRO RIFF

Note that this song utilizes a five-string bass, tuned down one half step. The Intro riff is based on the E minor pentatonic scale, with some odd timing thrown in for good measure. Newsted's initial entrance of the riff comes on the second beat of the measure. The first part of the riff uses a sort of an upper pedal tone on the D as the line descends the E minor pentatonic scale. Try to keep a finger planted on the D so it can sustain over the moving line. In measure 3, a full step bend on the G helps to give elasticity to the groove.

PRE-CHORUS LICK

In the second half of the Verse, Newsted pulls off an impressive array of bass licks. The groove starts in measure 1 with a descending line, implying the E blues and E natural minor scales. After an E minor turnaround lick at the end of measure 1 and steady, rhythmic Es on measure 2, Newsted lets loose in measure 3, using double stops (or, in this case, you could call them power chords) on and off the beats amidst the 16th notes, sextuplets, and 16th note triplets. He nails down the D feel with D power chords and quickly walks his way up to the F in beat 3, which includes a sextuplet figure scale pattern descending from F to C.

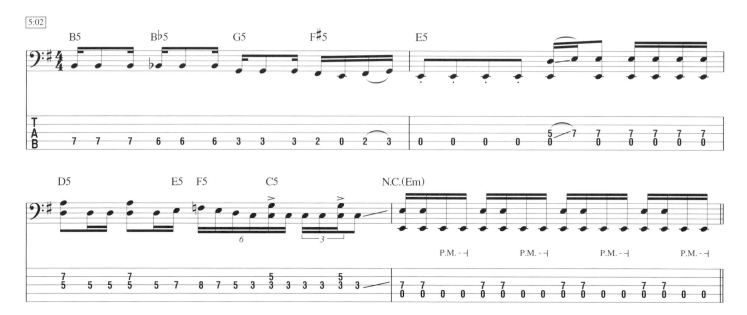

18

GUITAR SOLO SECTION

The guitar Solo section consists of a rhythmic pattern utilizing eighth and 16th notes. This riff is based on the E natural minor scale. For consistency's sake, practice the slides going up to the 7th fret E. The second half of the solo section changes the key focus to the dominant of E minor—B. Here, Newsted is able to use his low B string to add welcome depth to the sound.

COMING OUT RIFF

Coming out of the solo section, the whole band takes over, playing a variation on the main riff, accenting low Es and slamming into high Gs and G♯s. Feel free to slide up to the high notes and back down to the Es to add extra power to the groove. Measure 3 teases you with a short lick, pulling off from the G to the E. Keep your first finger planted on the E and lift off the G—this will help your tone to sustain. The next lick doubles the guitars—it is a series of slides going up the fingerboard, outlining the full E minor pentatonic scale.

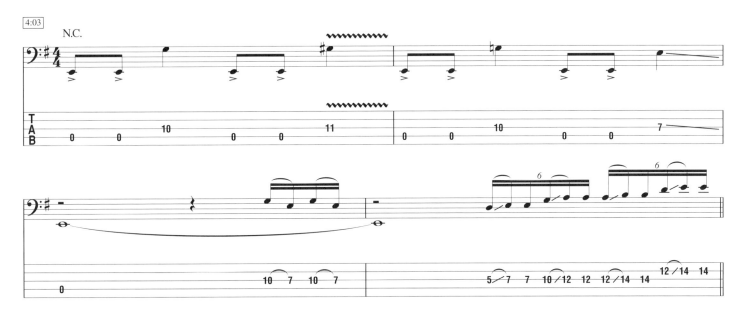

19

Bad Seed

Words and Music by
James Hetfield, Lars Ulrich and Kirk Hammett

OPENING RIFF

For this song, tune down one and a half steps if you'd like to match the pitches of the recording. The Intro riff is a scaled back version of a later riff with a more proactive bass line. Starting out, the bass is solid in its timing, locking in tightly with the bass drum on low Es while the guitars hammer out an E minor pentatonic riff. What makes this line cool is its combination of simplicity and functionality. The phrase ends with a hammered-on upper neighbor tone lick that teams up with the vocals.

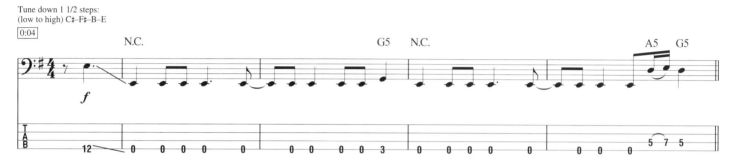

PROGRESSING RIFF

The Intro evolves into a meatier riff, utilizing bends and the E blues scale. The bass does some countering of the guitars, riding the low E with a driving rhythmic pattern; the guitars and bass meet up to double on the lick, which includes a half step bend on the A. This adds an extra bluesy feel to this heavy sound. Set up your hand positioning so you can catch the bend with your 3rd and 4th fingers while using your 1st finger to grab the G.

GUITAR SOLO SECTION

The guitar Solo section is a recap of the Intro riff, but the bass now doubles the guitar line note for note. The riff is an E minor pentatonic scale, which starts at the upper octave E and makes its way down the scale to the low, open E. A big chunk of the riff can be played using the box pattern fingering with your 1st and 3rd fingers. Because the scale has an odd number of notes in it, an extra low E is added to anticipate the next measure and even out the timing.

PRE-CHORUS VARIATION

At the end of the guitar Solo section, the band takes the riff and moves it to the key of A. The bass line continues to double the guitar line as in the previous section, which is a variation on the Verse feel.

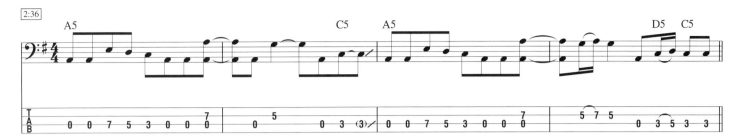

Words and Music by
James Hetfield, Lars Ulrich and Jason Newsted

Where the Wild Things Are

TRANSITION RIFF

Note that this song utilizes a five-string bass, tuned down one half step. This riff acts as a transition between the Verse and Chorus sections of the song. Doubling with the guitars, the groove goes back and forth between F and E, giving the riff a dark, exotic sound. The palm mute on the second half of beat 1 sets up the accented quarter note on beat 2. Come down hard on beat 2 and let the string ring out.

5 str. down 1/2 step:
(low to high) B♭–E♭–A♭–D♭–G♭

PRE-CHORUS RIFF

This riff is a great display of Newsted's ability to play a wide variety of double stops. This part moves temporarily to the key of D minor, making use of the ♯7th (C♯) and ♭6th (B♭) before finishing on a G5 chord.

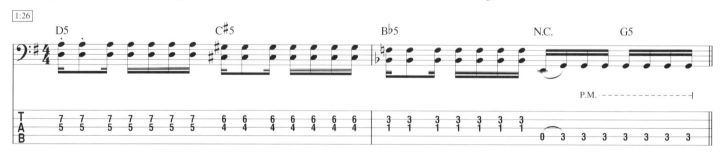

OCTAVE SLIDES

This short section is very cool but difficult. As the Pre-Chorus ends, Newsted hits more double stops, moving though different chords and intervals. Starting out with a power chord on E, he slides down to the 3rd fret C, maintaining the integrity of the double stop. After holding onto the C power chord, Newsted slides a finger up the neck to catch the C on the 8th fret, keeping his finger down on the D string for that lower octave. He finishes with octave Bs and then slides down to Gs. This is all harder to play than it may seem. Make sure to keep your fingers firmly on the strings to keep their vibrations going, and in position to arrive at the next stop cleanly.

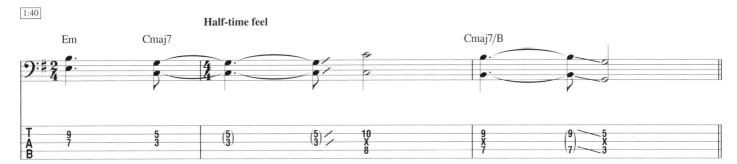

BRIDGE RIFF (PART 1)

This section shows Newsted pulling off some tricky rhythm patterns. As most of the rhythmic content is based on the drum groove, the melodic content recalls the transition riff mentioned earlier, using the half step E-to-F groove. These notes are played high up on the fingerboard, giving you plenty of room to slide, if you'd like. The high notes are accented with the drums. Take special notice of beat 2, where the accent is always coupled with a cymbal crash.

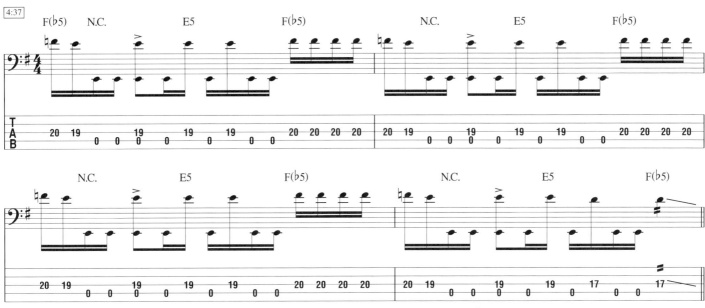

BRIDGE RIFF (PART 2)

The second half of the Bridge section has Newsted playing the bass line down low. Notice how the low Es not only mirror the drums, but also eventually have the same function as the high Es in the first part of this section. In measure 4, he plays a brilliant E minor pentatonic lick, sequencing the scale from the upper octave. As the line moves on, the low Es take rhythmic control, paralleling the drums and focusing on the second beat of each measure with accents. Muffled notes fill the spaces in between to heavy out the sound. Play these by palm muting the string with your right hand and fully muting the string with your left hand to completely eliminate the pitch, creating a thud-like sound.

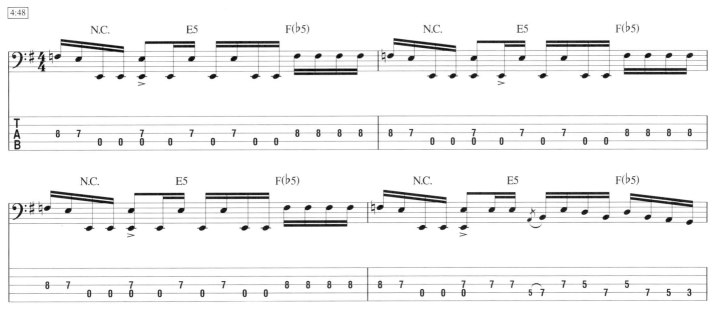

Prince Charming

Words and Music by
James Hetfield and Lars Ulrich

MAIN RIFF

Tune down one half step for this song if you'd like to match the pitches of the recording. The main riff of the song shows off a solid foundation for the guitar line. Newsted plays riding eighth notes through the section, showing how important a simple but steady line can be. Between some chords, he throws in chromatic passing tones to smooth out the transitions. Each chord change is also anticipated by an eighth note—this accentuates the timing of the guitar melody line.

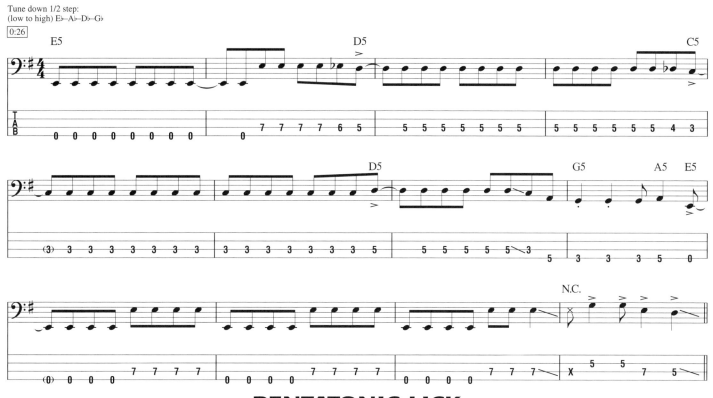

PENTATONIC LICK

In the Chorus section, at the end of the second ending, Newsted plays an interesting pentatonic lick in E minor. As it goes down the scale in stepwise motion, it finishes with running 4ths which help set up the upcoming guitar solo section in F♯ minor.

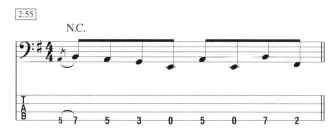

GUITAR SOLO SECTION

This section is a variation on the Verse riff, using flowing eighth notes and a short, moving line juxtaposed on top. The low F♯s act as a pedal to the occasional moving line that dances around the F♯ minor pentatonic scale—keep the running pedal notes as steady as possible when playing the moving part of the line.

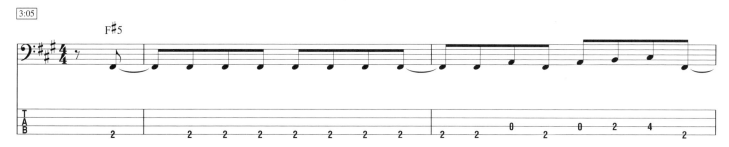

25

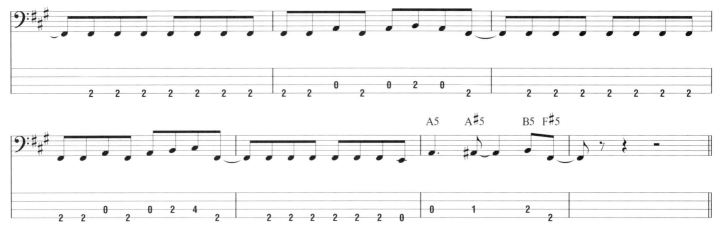

INTERLUDE

This section has the same steady feel as the others but now is a bit more active in its approach. While the eighth notes are still there, Newsted wisely chooses to link up the low Es with the bass drums for punchiness while the higher octave Es act as a support system for the blazing guitar melody. This technique of playing two roles is used by bass players in all styles. While the bass is linked up with the drums, it mimics the melody in its higher octave—all just through one note.

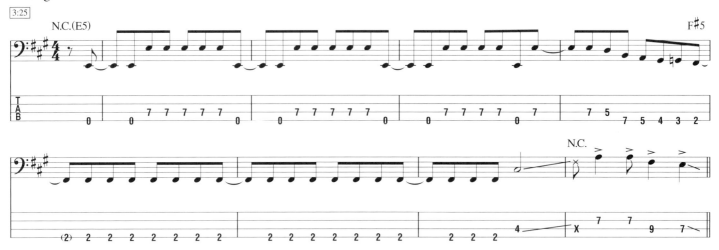

HALF TIME BENDS

At the culmination of the half time section, Newsted gets crazy with some intense note bending. After sliding to the bluesy C♮ from F♯, he proceeds to bend the C up a whole step and holds it there for most of the second measure. It may be necessary to use all of your left-hand fingers to make this gnarly bend happen.

OUTRO RIFF

The Outro riff has a cool spot where the low E acts as a pedal tone under a moving, bluesy line. This riff is yet another variation on the main riff of the song. Playing the moving line on a separate string can help the clarity of the low Es.

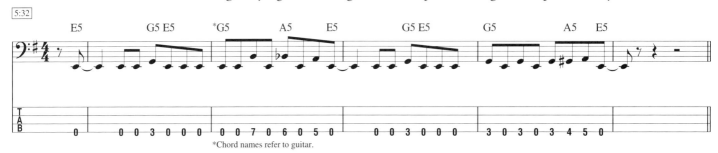

*Chord names refer to guitar.

Low Man's Lyric

Words and Music by
James Hetfield and Lars Ulrich

CHORUS RIFF (PART 1)

For this song, tune down one half step if you want to match the pitches of the recording. The Chorus riff has Newsted demonstrating some excellent slide work. Starting on the 12th fret A, he waits just before the chord change and plays a 10th fret G, which slides down to the E on the same string—the G is a good note choice because it is the 3rd of the E minor chord. As the progression moves back to the A minor chord, he plays a grace note F# to the G and then goes back to the A; the G acts as a bridge between the two chords. The progression then moves to E minor; Newsted uses a B to slide to the E (this B is also a good choice because it is the 5th of the E minor chord). When playing a slide, hit the note and then time the slide so it reaches its destination *in time*. Shoot for a smooth and easy feel between notes.

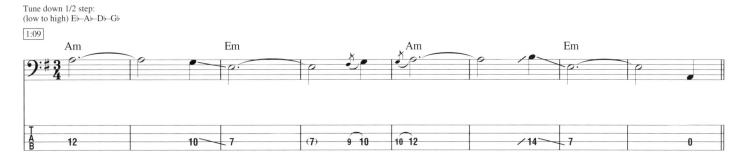

CHORUS RIFF (PART 2)

As the Chorus winds down, the progression stops on the V chord of E minor (B5) and holds there for the big finish. As the line stays on the B, the bass is right on with the drumbeat, mimicking the bass drum. Newsted plays double stops (B power chords) at the end for a cool effect, using them rhythmically.

VERSE RIFF

The Verse section is in A major—a different key than the Chorus. Many of the bass licks have more of a pentatonic feel, utilizing C♮ and G♮. In the third Verse, there is good use of slides and some walking tones to help the line move. At the end of the phrase, Newsted plays a figure that recurs in every Verse; recurring figures like these help to bring a "familiar" aspect to various parts of the song and give the bass line a distinctive voice.

CHORUS VARIATIONS

Newsted pulls out some groove chops as he makes his way through this Chorus. All kinds of techniques are used, as the song is cruising at this point. In the second measure, there's a muted note to a slide, which is used as a transition to an E minor chord—this figure really brings out a kind of "swing feel" as it seems to be bouncing through the groove. Measure 4 utilizes grace notes. Make sure each grace note is played so that each target note lands squarely on the beat. Measure 9's triplet gives off a bold and powerful feel as it sets up a climax.

Attitude

Words and Music by
James Hetfield and Lars Ulrich

PRE-CHORUS RIFF

Tune down one half step if you'd like to match the pitches of the recording for this song. In the Verse section, the harmony goes to a D minor sound for a short time. Newsted hammers out eighth notes to keep the flow moving forward over the half time drum feel. As the progression goes to the C5, the rhythm has a more syncopated feel, matching the hits of the drums. At the end of each two-measure phrase, Newsted sets up the D5 chord with a solid pentatonic lick using the notes A and C with the implied harmony being the v chord of D.

INTERLUDE SECTION (PART 1)

In a different half time feel during the Interlude, Newsted uses harmonics to double the rhythm guitar mutes. As he does this, he not only reinforces the guitars, but also opens up the sound. Harmonics are overtones of a string's pitch that, when played, can create actual pitches that go way beyond the natural range of the bass. You can get a harmonic when you place a finger directly on top of a fret, but not fully pushing down on the string; the most easily attained harmonics are on the 5th, 7th, and 12th frets.

INTERLUDE SECTION (PART 2)

At the end of the Interlude section, Newsted shows us another interesting technique involving two voices being played simultaneously on the bass, but it's not a true double stop. The low E and its 7th fret octave are first struck together, and on the second half of beat 3, the higher E is bent up a whole step and is released at the beginning of the next measure. This is repeated in the next two measures before a big slide takes us out. The high E must sustain through the three measures, so giving the note a little vibrato can help. Make sure to bend the string away from the low E to allow the open string to ring.

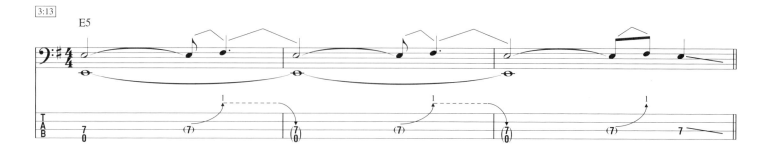

SOLO SECTION RIFF

During the guitar Solo, a variation of the Verse riff is brought back. Outlining the E blues scale, the riff starts on the "blue note" B♭ and goes through the G before ending up on the E. The last measure in this example ends with a riff that stays true to the rhythmic plan laid out in the previous measures—the difference here is that Newsted throws down a lick that descends the E minor pentatonic scale.

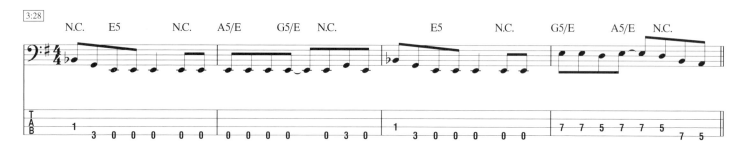

Words and Music by
James Hetfield, Lars Ulrich and Kirk Hammett

Fixxxer

OPENING RIFF

Note that this song utilizes a five-string bass, tuned down one half step. After a short guitar Intro, the bass comes on strong with a solid groove bearing many licks. One can really hear Newsted's Geezer Butler (Black Sabbath) influence. The riff and licks go back and forth between the E natural minor and the E minor pentatonic scales. The second ending shows a classic use of the minor pentatonic. The third and fourth endings use the minor pentatonic above that 7th fret E on the A string, showing a part of the extended upper range of the scale. The riff finishes with a descending sequence pattern using the natural minor scale.

5 str. down 1/2 step:
(low to high) B♭–E♭–A♭–D♭–G♭

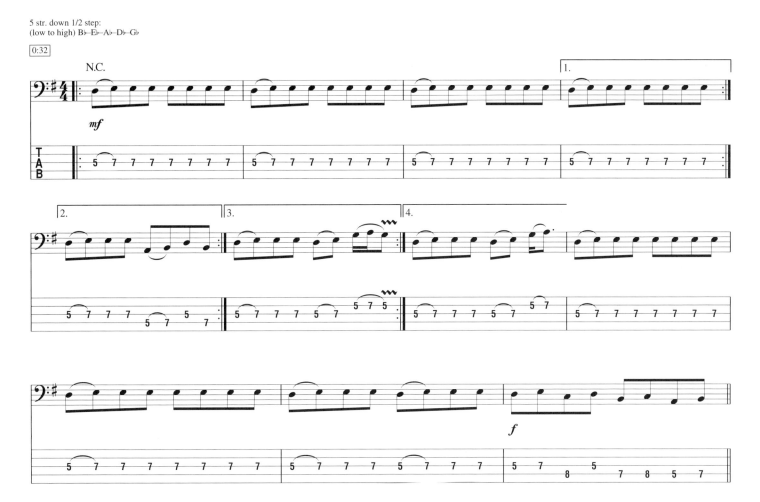

HALF TIME FEEL

In the second part of the Intro, Newsted counters the guitar line with a tasteful use of the lower range of the bass, taking notes down when the guitar line moves higher. This is a great effect because it gives the line a wider spectrum of sound. It first happens in the second measure on the low F and again in the fourth measure on the lick over the D5. This riff comes back later in the key of F♯ minor.

31

SOLO SECTION LICK

At the end of the guitar Solo section, we're back in the key of E minor (after a section in F♯ minor), and Newsted pulls out a cool set of licks. After the held low E, one of the themes of the Intro lick is brought back, played in the upper range of the bass. Newsted then unleashes a descending minor pentatonic lick off the high E. The grace note Ds give the lick a bluesy feel.

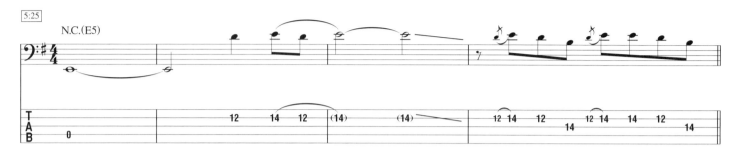

INTERLUDE LICK

During the Interlude, Newsted plays a cool and diverse sounding lick. After holding steady on the Es, he pulls out a lick based on the C minor pentatonic scale. This juxtaposing of keys gives off a very striking and colorful sound; it works because C is a note in the E minor scale, and he simply uses that as his base for the minor pentatonic scale. The half step bend on the F♮ helps to bring us back to E minor.

BRIDGE RIFF

The Bridge section is driven by the bass—you can really hear Newsted's feel and tone shine through. The riff uses a combination of the E minor and E blues scales. Starting on the low E, it jumps directly up to the octave and makes its way down via the minor scale, skipping notes to compensate for timing. The low E anticipates the next measure by an eighth note for some syncopation. The riff ends by doubling the guitars with a bluesy half step bend on the A to the "blue note" B♭.

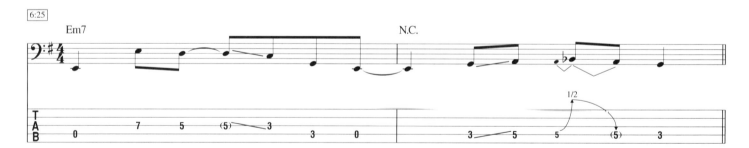

GARAGE INC.

Words and Music by
Philip Parris Lynott, Brian Michael Downey and Eric Bell

Whiskey in the Jar

GETTING CONNECTED

Tune your bass down one whole step if you'd like to match the pitches of the recording. Jason does a fine job of both setting a strong and stable groove and connecting the chords of the Verse together. The rests on the strong beats of 2 and 4 give the snare drum space to ring freely. This rhythm pattern is present through most of the song. As the G5 chord goes into the E5 chord, Jason connects with an ascending lick using the E minor pentatonic scale to set up the E5—the bass really helps to distinguish the sounds of G major and its relative minor (E minor). Moving on, between the E5 and the C5, Jason uses the passing tone D to help link the chords; he does the same from the C5 to the G5 with the A.

Tune down 1 step:
(low to high) D–G–C–F

PENTATONIC RIFF

These are classic examples of the pentatonic minor scale in action. As the Chorus plays out, the mood is heightened by a pentatonic riff starting on low C and ascending the scale to the upper octave. Newsted chooses to play the riff going up the neck, playing the upper octave on the 10th fret of the D string. By this point, the mood of the groove is peaking, its energy at full tilt. Finishing out the Chorus, Newsted descends the pentatonic scale staying up on the neck, culminating with a giant slide from the D on the E string. This is a great place to do the slide; it is high on the neck and the D is the perfect note to set up the upcoming G5 chord.

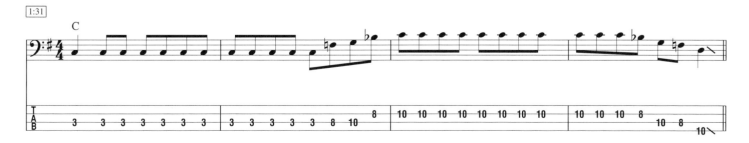

THE FISH IS A-ROARIN'

The fourth Verse has a more spacious feel than the previous three, which allows for more expressive bass lines. Newsted uses the vocals as cues to craft cool rhythmic variations, giving the bass a more active, lyrical role. This first happens in measure 1—after playing long notes on the G, he uses an eighth note anticipation into the second measure on the word "fishin'." A similar situation arises two measures later, at the culmination of the first half of the Verse—this time there are two anticipations, both on G. The first one anticipates the third beat of the measure, helping to accentuate the word "cannonball," and the second one anticipates the next measure, emphasizing the lyric "a-roarin'."

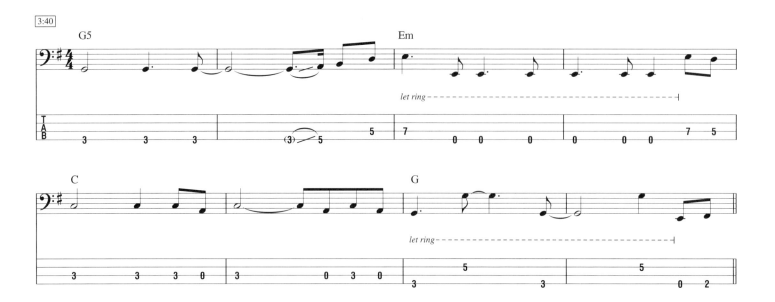

Last Caress

Words and Music by
Glenn Danzig

I–IV–V

The Verse riff uses the standard I–IV–V chord progression in the key of C major. Notice how the IV and V chords (F5 and G5, respectively) add emphasis to the running eighth notes of the I chord (C5).

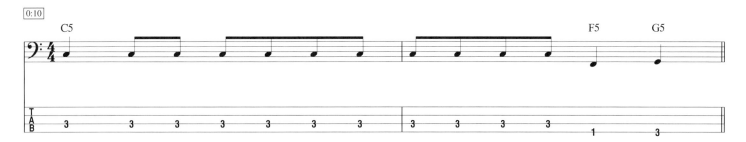

THE SET-UP

The rhythm in this passage is a precursor to what's to come rhythmically in the Chorus; it is slightly different than the Verse due to the tie on the upbeat of beat 2. The chord progression also changes—it starts on a IV (F5) chord and rather than going to the V (G5) chord, the line moves to the ii (D5) chord. Notice that in measure 2, Newsted sets up the I chord by using an upper neighbor tone off the D to move downward through that note until he reaches the root of the C5 chord in the third measure.

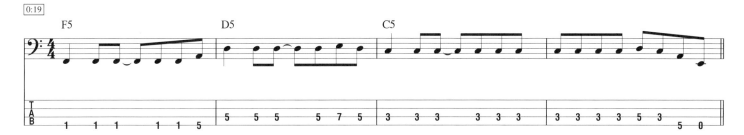

CHORUS GROOVE

The Chorus groove is much like the previous transitional section. Harmonically, in the second measure, rather than going to the D5, it goes to the G5 chord coming from the F5. The third and fourth measures take a different turn; over the chords that descend from the C, Newsted uses the low open E to help drive the line home. A lot of times, players use the open E as a "feel thing" to help give a line some extra punch.

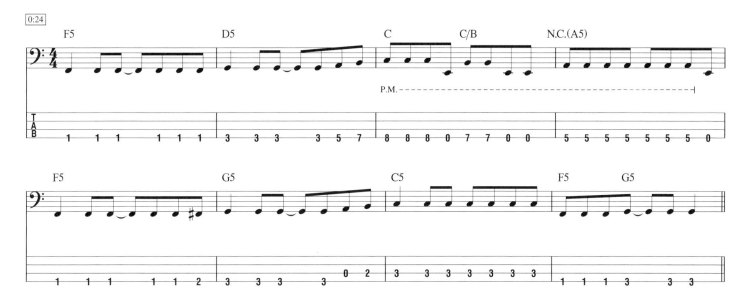

Am I Evil?

Words and Music by
Sean Harris and Brian Tatler

SLIDIN' INTRO

Once the main riff of the song has started, Burton shows his bluesy side using the pentatonic and blues scales to help push the riff along. What makes this riff so cool is his use of slides. In measure 2, Burton uses a grace note slide from D to E to help bump out a lick using the E minor pentatonic scale; notice how this scale works over different chords in the progression. The lick beginning at the end of measure 3 starts out with sliding eighth notes on E to D and then slides back and makes its way down the E blues scale, setting up the equally bluesy main riff.

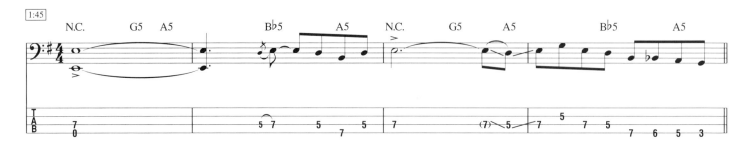

VERSE RIFF

This riff uses the blues scale in E. It demonstrates excellent syncopation, accenting the ascending scale both on and off the beats. This riff also shows up in the Verse with the B blues scale.

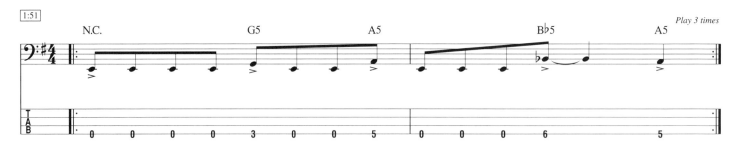

BLUES SCALE GOING UP

Once the main riff has been established, Burton uses the E blues scale in an ascending pattern to help introduce the vocal entrance. This lick occurs in the same spot in the measure as the previous lick, showing that you can use many different variations over the same chord progression. This one starts in the middle of the scale on the note A. It works well because it acts as a natural continuation of the main riff, which climbs the E blues scale.

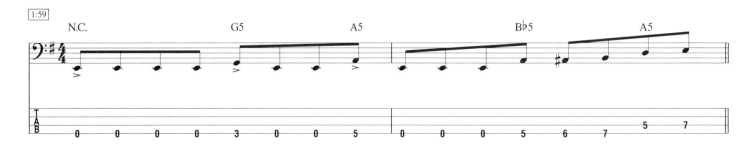

COVERING SOME SPACE

Here is a classic example showing the agility of Cliff Burton. Under the driving rhythm of the A5 chord, he utilizes A octaves, covering a huge amount of distance on the fingerboard at a lightening pace. This shows a fantastic display of mixed rhythms, going between eighth notes and triplets much like the song "The Four Horsemen." Burton uses the A pentatonic minor scale to finish out the lick, ending in the middle of the scale on an E. This is a great set up for the main riff of the Bridge, which is in E.

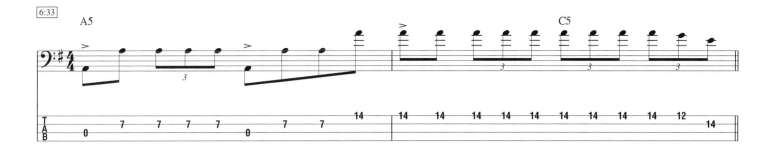

BRIDGE RIFF

The main riff of the Bridge shows great insight into the quirkiness and complexities of Metallica's rhythmic style. It starts again with that dynamic display of mixed rhythm, using eighth notes and triplets together. The band constantly changes the flow of the riff by surprising you with stops and stutters. At the end of the second measure, they hit you hard with an accented dotted quarter note on D, bringing a temporary pause. Two measures later, they use quarter note triplets to stutter the groove, showing a cool diversity of feels.

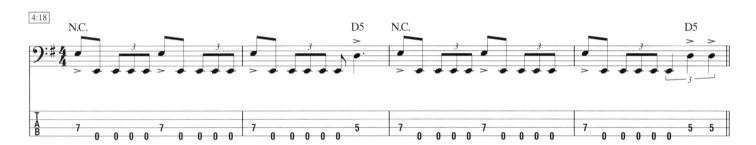

Words and Music by
Ian Jones, Brian Ross and Jim Sirotto

Blitzkrieg

POLYRHYTHMIC CHORUS GROOVE

The Chorus groove for "Blitzkrieg" is extremely syncopated, and it will take some practice for it to feel comfortable. The accents are constantly shifting around, giving the groove a *polyrhythmic feel* (the feeling of two different meters at the same time, such as 3 against 2). Although the groove is in 4/4 time, the phrasing has a "3 feel." If you accent the D hammer-on, you will feel the time shifts, as this gesture always happens in a different spot in the measure. The open E is essential as a filler of sound and a reminder that, though the myriad of chords, the groove is still in E minor.

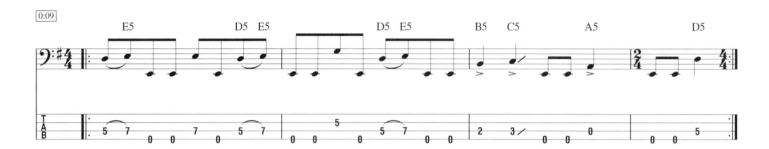

DEVELOPMENTAL SECTION (PART 1)—HALF TIME FEEL

In what could be considered the developmental section of the song, Metallica puts the brakes on the driving eighth note rhythms and creates a section full of space. Burton accents and holds onto the roots of each chord. In measure 3, he plays a descending E minor scale, purposely omitting the C to help set up the C5 chord. As he transitions into each chord, the bass and drums take the lead by riffing together. In measures 5 through 6, while using the same concepts seen in the previous E minor lick, Burton shadows the drum fills to create a wall of rhythmic and melodic sound.

DEVELOPMENTAL SECTION (PART 2)—SPEED AND POWER

The developmental section continues with Burton laying down lightening fast 16ths at the original tempo over the E5–C5 chord progression. The E minor scale is used in full effect as the line starts on the tonic of the scale and ascends stepwise with a brief replay of the G to help set up the C5 chord. Once on the C, the scale is then descended in the same way. This is a good example of how the same scale can essentially work for two different chords.

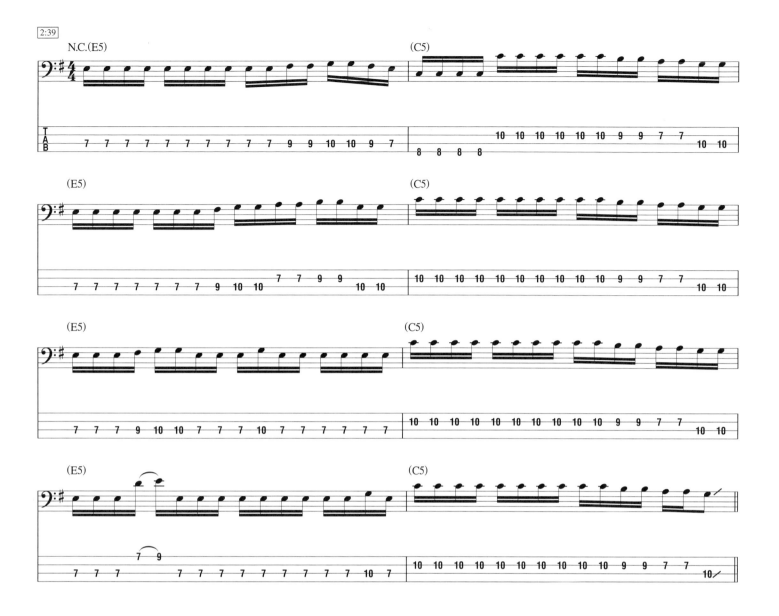

DEVELOPMENTAL SECTION (PART 3)—AWESOME FINALE

Here the band shows their musical mastery as they combine the original riff and the developmental section chord progression to perform a variation before taking us back to the Verse groove and out of the song. Burton uses a fantastic array of E octaves, choosing the higher E to accentuate the rhythm guitar part. This effect causes the upper octave to switch back and forth between the strong and weak parts of each beat.

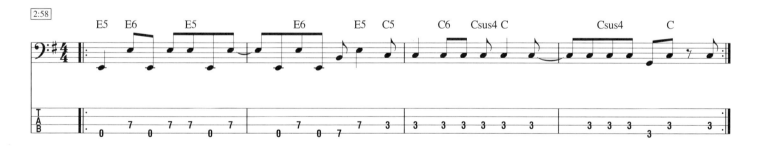

Words and Music by
Anthony Bourge, John Burke Shelley and Raymond Phillips

Breadfan

INTRO RIFF

The Intro riff is based on a three-note pattern (D–E–E) spread out over two measures. Each time the pattern comes back around it starts at a different spot in the measure, suggesting a polyrhythmic 3-against-2 feel. An eighth note is added to the last pattern in order for the two-measure phrase to be completed. In measures 3 and 4, the second phrase begins in the same way. It utilizes the three-note pattern but quickly resolves itself to finish off with a descending E minor pentatonic scale. Notice in measure 3 how the D grace note implies the D–E–E pattern, but also sets up the end of the riff.

POWER STOPS

In this section, Newsted plays double stops to add some extra heaviness to the already heavy guitars. Following the chord progression, the root of the chord is the lower note, and the 5th of the chord is the higher. This is a technique that, when used tastefully, can create a very cool sound.

PENTATONIC LICKS

The half time feel starts with running minor pentatonic licks doubling the guitars, going down the neck. Each scale pattern starts on the lower neighbor note of the scale, resolving to the tonic, then going to a higher note and resolving again to the tonic. This widely used pentatonic lick is a great example of how the same pattern can be used at different places on the neck and doesn't always have to start on the tonic. Stop the string with your left hand at the end of measures 1 and 2 to create a non-pitched sound when attacked. A curious line ends the riff each time, implying the V chord of E minor (B) and making its way back to the licks again via F#, G, and G#. The last time through this riff, this line sets up the upcoming A nicely.

THE SLIDE

Newsted uses slides to culminate the end of the first phrase in the slow guitar Solo section. Slides are difficult to play well on the bass—it takes a lot of practice to make them sound natural. The start of each Em7 chord is in a tight lock with the drums, nailing the bass drum pattern of a dotted quarter note and eighth note. He uses the octave E to hold steady on the backbeat of the snare. Newsted goes to the 5th of the chord, choosing to play it low on the neck in order to achieve the slide effect, as he uses the entire quarter note to slide from the 2nd to the 7th fret. The B is a great note to choose, given that it is the 5th of E, making it a first-choice move to set up the octave. As he lingers on the high E, he again uses a quarter note to slide down to the low F, which chromatically sets up the low E.

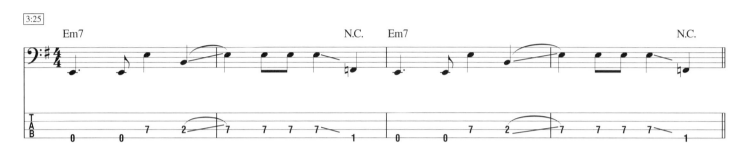

No Leaf Clover

Words and Music by
James Hetfield and Lars Ulrich

VERSE RIFF

Note that this song utilizes a five-string bass, tuned down one half step. The Verse riff is full of complex rhythm patterns. Stealing patterns from the Intro, the song has a definite sense of unity between the parts. The bass supports the chord progression, but the bulk of the line remains tight with the drums, mirroring the bass drum on beats 1 and 3, while also catching the 16th note bass drum hits against a wall of guitar. Harmonically, the line moves through the key of E minor, from which a good number of his licks derive. At the end of measures 1 and 3, Newsted throws in a 16th note triplet lick off the B setting up the main riff, soon to be answered by the snare drum at the end of the next measure.

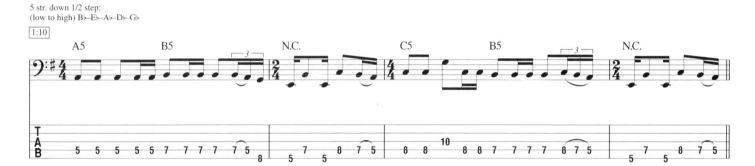

CHORUS RIFF

The Chorus riff is great example of Newsted's ability to create a fully independent line. While each measure opens up with the same rhythm shadowing the bass drum (eighth note–quarter note), the second half of the each measure shows Newsted taking chances and exercising the restraint that only an experienced player can. In the first and third measures, he uses the E minor scale, playing arpeggios to help direct his line to each upcoming Am chord, where he then lets the half note A ride. But the second and fourth measures are a whole different trip—measure 2 finishes over the A minor chord with a very tasty lick off the E minor scale, starting on the C and descending to the G to set up the E minor chord in the next measure (the same thing occurs an octave lower in the last Chorus). This works because of the common tones between the keys of A minor and E minor.

TAG IT ON

After the second ending of the Chorus, at the Bridge, Newsted takes some liberties in his line, playing more melodically within the rhythmic motives of the song. The second measure is all over the place, hitting E octaves until he uses the minor pentatonic scale to seamlessly connect the E minor chord with the B7 chord. Then, he uses his trademark grace note approach, ornamenting the B7 chord via its ♭7, A. Each measure contains vital rhythmic figures that keep the continuity of the feel alive while still managing to maintain an independent voice. Measure 3 builds with intensity as he plays a 16th note C over the D chord on beat 3 (resolving immediately) and sets up the B5 with a 16th note triplet through the D.

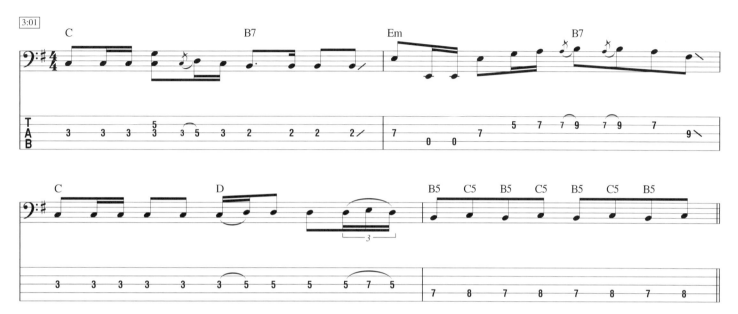

GUITAR SOLO SECTION

This section harkens back to the beginning of the tune, bringing back the opening riff. Newsted, using the pentatonic minor scale, expands upon the riff in the first part of several measures. Measure 3 starts with a lick à la Black Sabbath, using parts of the E minor pentatonic scale to help stabilize the E minor feel. Measure 4 is another pentatonic riff with an added chromatic (D♯) between the D and E to create a bluesy feel and an even stronger push to E.

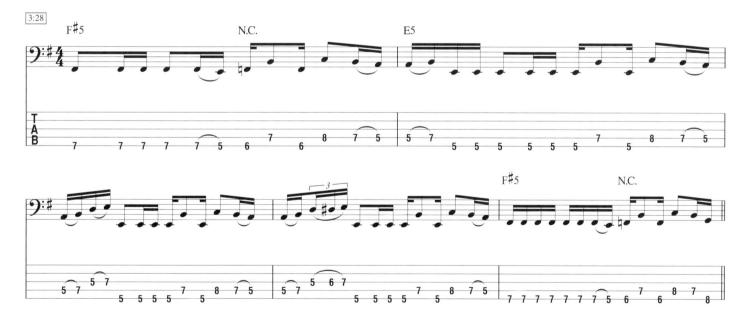

Words and Music by
James Hetfield and Lars Ulrich

– Human

HEAVY RIFF

If you'd like to match the pitches of the recording, tune your bass to drop D down a half step. The bass and guitars double the 6/4 time opening and Chorus riff; it has an extremely heavy vibe, loosely recalling the vintage Black Sabbath song "Into the Void." Using vibrato to intensify the feel, the riff cascades down the D blues scale, starting on the 5th, going through the ♯4 (the blue note) before stopping on the minor 3rd. Measure 2 takes an unexpected melodic turn by adding the note E to the line, expanding the sound of the scale and setting up a strong pull to the ♭3. This riff also foreshadows upcoming riffs with its use of rhythmic displacement of the beat, putting the emphasis on the "weak" parts of the measure (the "and" of beat 2, plus beats 4 and 6).

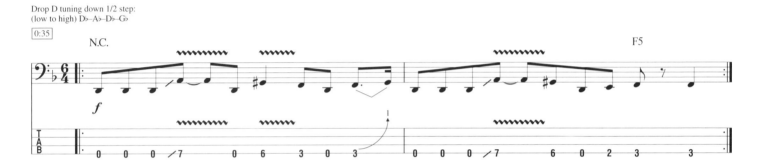

BRIDGE RIFF

This riff takes its cue from the previous riff, displacing the higher octave Ds to the weak parts of beats. The first phrase ends with a lick using the D blues scale.

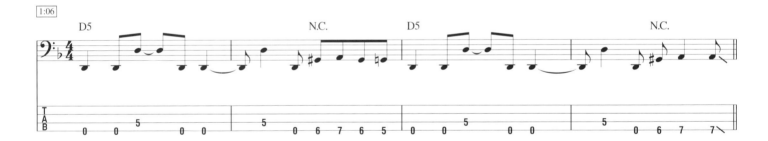

VERSE RIFF

Newsted does a fine job connecting chords with passing tones as the line slowly rises; these tones occur naturally in the scale of D minor. Practice the scale, paying attention to how each note flows into the next, and then compare this to the chord progression. The line culminates on the G5 chord, with an A used to set up the D5 chord in the next measure.

SOLO SECTION

Rhythmic displacement reaches its apex at this point. Driving the sound with octaves, the bass line fools you with its polyrhythmic on-the-beat/off-the-beat figures; you can't quite tell where each measure begins or ends. But the riff rhythmically "stabilizes" every third measure before it finally finishes with a descending D blues scale.

MISSION: IMPOSSIBLE 2 SOUNDTRACK

Words and Music by
James Hetfield and Lars Ulrich

I Disappear

VERSE RIFF

The Verse riff starts out with an eighth note anticipation to beat 1 and follows with offbeat Es that are placed with precision. The Es match the bass drum hits, while the snare drum fills in the spaces left on beats 2 and 4. If you can really feel the strong pulse of the quarter note beat, the execution of this tricky riff will fall into place. In measure 5, Newsted plays a mammoth slide off the G and crashes down onto the open E on beat 2, resuming the groove. The riff finishes with a moving E minor line, played on the open E string.

CHORUS RIFF (PART 1)

This moody Chorus riff also features plenty of anticipations of each chord, but this time some are not tied but articulated for a better effect. Newsted demonstrates a fine use of passing tones and slides to connect the chords; this effect is achieved by keeping the line on the E string and utilizing the length of the string to get the progression.

SOLO SECTION RIFF

The guitar Solo section starts out with a bass lick on the open E first heard in the beginning of the song. Notice how Newsted opts for the low E instead of the higher one—this gives the lick a cool dynamic effect by filling out the sound and range. It finishes with a short turn between the D and E. The bulk of the section is based on the second opening riff, only now the bass drives the progression, holding steady eighth notes. The progression is centered in E minor as well, and Newsted closes the phrase accordingly with an E minor pentatonic lick that culminates on the 7th fret E.

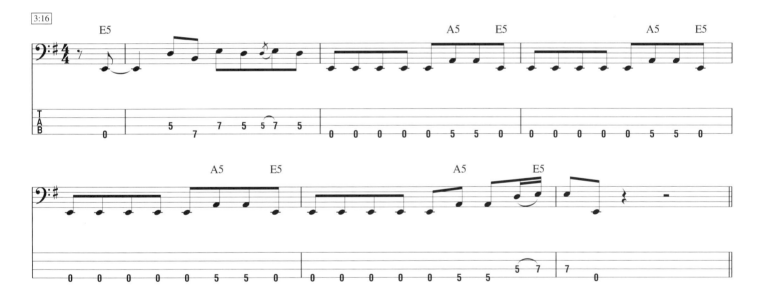

ST. ANGER

Words and Music by
James Hetfield, Lars Ulrich, Kirk Hammett and Bob Rock

Copyright © 2003 Creeping Death Music (ASCAP), EMI Blackwood (Canada) Music Ltd.
and Mahina Hoku Publishing
All Rights for EMI Blackwood (Canada) Music Ltd. and Mahina Hoku Publishing
Controlled and Administered by EMI Blackwood Music Inc.
International Copyright Secured   All Rights Reserved

Frantic

INTRO SECTION

Note that this song utilizes a five-string bass in drop D tuning, down one whole step. The Intro section of this song has all the aggression one could possibly stand. This riff uses the D blues scale, accenting the tritone "blue note" on beat 1. This has a temporary resolution to G on beat 3, while keeping its key center via the 16th note Ds. The accents on the downbeats also allow the following 16ths on beats 2 and 4 to flow easier. Notice how beats 1 and 3 also reinforce the vocal line that will eventually be sung over this part.

WICKED GROOVE

One of the catch phrases of the tune, this riff could also been seen as a variation on the Intro riff. The tied eighth notes create an offbeat call-and-response feel against the backbeat of Ulrich's fast, driving snare. On the DVD, Trujillo plays this riff up above the 12th fret. Playing in this area of the bass gives your tone more "girth" because of the fat strings. Geezer Butler used this technique to help get his distinctive tones on the early Black Sabbath albums.

THE CALM AMIDST THE STORM

The men of Metallica are master mood setters, able to calm the vibe amidst a storm of aggression. Notice how the 8th notes in the line have more room to breathe. This is due to the opening up of the drums' half time feel. The harmony moves to the G chord, making use of the F minor pentatonic scale. The line holds steady on the root of the chord, going to its lower neighbor (F) and upper 4th (C). This is a common technique in drop tuning because of the hand positioning. Notice on beats 2 and 4 how the offbeat 8th notes maintain a tight lock with the bass drum.

OUTRO RIFF

This driving riff makes for a raucous ending if ever there was one. Made up of mainly the root and ♭7th of the D5 chord, it sits well with Ulrich's drum groove. Make sure that slide on the last note is a quick one—you don't want to be lingering on that D after the rest of the band has finished having its say.

Words and Music by
James Hetfield, Lars Ulrich, Kirk Hammett and Bob Rock

St. Anger

OPENING RIFF

Note that this song utilizes a five-string bass in drop D and A tuning, down one whole step. The opening riff for the song is a heavily accented chromatic line that is harder to play than you might think, given the tempo of the feel. Make sure to organize the note pattern in your left hand at a slow tempo before speeding it up.

5 str. drop D and A tuning, down 1 step:
(low to high) G–C–G–C–F

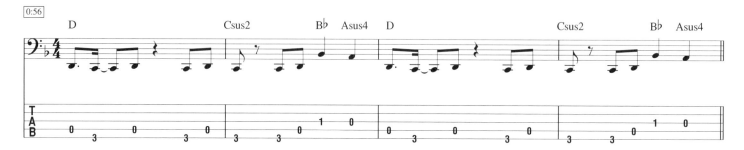

VERSE RIFF

The Verse's implied simplicity is masked by a deceiving complexity. The riff is dead on with the drums, outlining the D chord by going back and forth between the low D and C, before moving through the Csus2, B♭, and Asus4 chords. What is really interesting about this groove is its phrasing; the drum beat echoes anything but a normal 4/4 beat, continually placing the snare on the weak part of the beat. The best way to keep up with this riff without losing your feel is to really get into the rhythmic phrasing of the drum beat and play right on top of it.

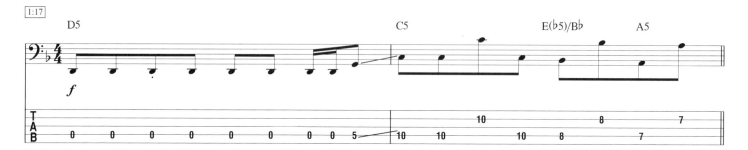

PRE-CHORUS RIFF

The bass keeps a rock solid feel over the chiming guitars. Staying very true to the harmonic progression, Rock slams eighth note Ds over the first measure before sliding up the neck for the rest of the descending chords. He plays octaves through the moving line to help stabilize the chords and cut through the guitars.

CHORUS RIFF

The Chorus riff stays on eighth notes while following the chord progression. On the DVD, Trujillo doubles the guitars' lightning fast 16th notes using his three-finger "tarantula" technique—alternate picking the strings between his index and middle fingers and his ring finger (there are some good close-ups of this).

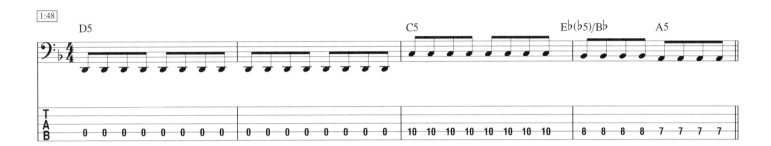

Words and Music by
James Hetfield, Lars Ulrich, Kirk Hammett and Bob Rock

Copyright © 2003 Creeping Death Music (ASCAP), EMI Blackwood (Canada) Music Ltd.
and Mahina Hoku Publishing
All Rights for EMI Blackwood (Canada) Music Ltd. and Mahina Hoku Publishing
Controlled and Administered by EMI Blackwood Music Inc.
International Copyright Secured   All Rights Reserved

Some Kind of Monster

OPENING RIFF (PART 1)

Note that this song utilizes a five-string bass in drop D tuning, down one whole step. The opening riff calls back to early Black Sabbath with a bluesy, heavy, plodding feel. The riff goes up the D minor pentatonic scale, stopping at G before starting over again. This is another three-note phrase that keeps repeating until its cycle starts over.

OPENING RIFF (PART 2)

The bass creates its own space by countering the melody of the guitars with a riff of its own. The riff is based on the D pentatonic minor scale, using a good deal of grace notes against the tonic. While the shape of the groove stays the same throughout the eight-measure section, Rock throws in slight variations every other bar to provide a cool complement to the original. Compare measure 1 with measures 2, 4, 6, and 8. When playing grace notes, make sure to play the actual grace note just before the beat so the intended note is played on the beat. Also, keep your 1st finger planted so that the grace note goes into the intended note as smoothly as any hammer-on.

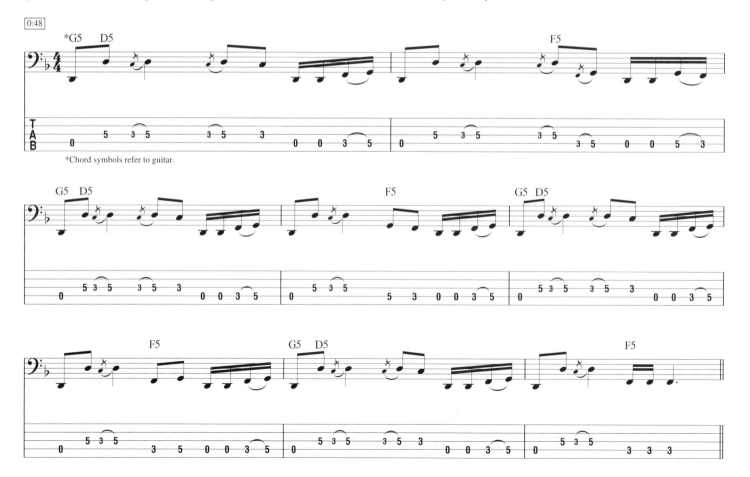

OPENING RIFF (PART 3)

This two-part riff is the precursor to the Verse riff. The rhythm is very syncopated, offsetting the beat in the middle of the measure. This first part shows the riff with just octaves plus grace notes, doubling the guitars exactly.

The second part has the bass utilizing more of a varied range of notes in different places. Take note of the F♯ harmonic at the end of the first measure. Be sure to place your left-hand finger directly on top of the fret to stop the string, but do not push down completely.

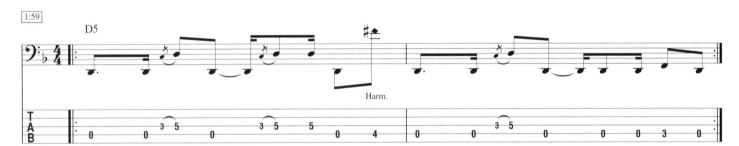

Words and Music by
James Hetfield, Lars Ulrich, Kirk Hammett and Bob Rock

Dirty Window

OPENING RIFF

Note that this song utilizes a five-string bass in drop D tuning, down one half step. This opening riff takes me back to the middle section of "Into the Void" from the album *Masters of Reality* by Black Sabbath. Very heavy and very low—and very fast—this riff borrows directly from the D blues scale. The three-note pattern uses the first half of the scale, while in the second measure the riff uses the other half of the scale to finish. Beware of the fingering issues that can occur as a result of drop D tuning. Be ready to hit the 6th fret A♭ from the 5th fret high D.

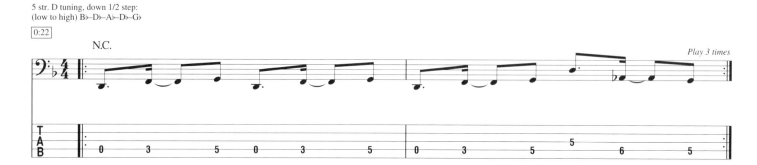

PRE-CHORUS RIFF (PART 1)

The Verse riff uses the D blues scale as well, but finishes with a curious lick at the end of the two-bar phrase. The first measure uses the three-note pattern discussed earlier, which stops to let the vocals have their say. The musical answer is a fully diminished 7th arpeggio based on D with an added G to keep the integrity of the three-note pattern. Make sure to play the last three notes as a hammer-on/pull-off to make the note transition smooth.

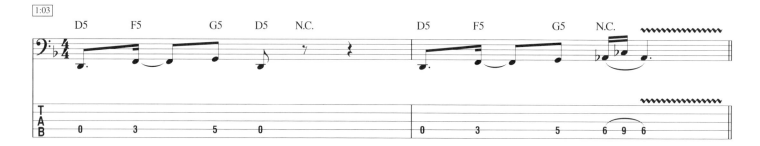

PRE-CHORUS RIFF (PART 2)

Here, the previous riff is transposed up a minor 3rd to F. The trick to playing this riff successfully is to have good peripheral vision happening so you can travel up the neck to the higher frets at the end.

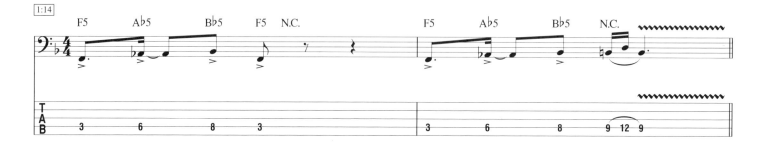

PALM MUTING FOR EFFECT

At the end of the Pre-Chorus, the rhythmic, three-note pattern is played in a muted style to emphasize the words, giving off the feeling of "slamming my gavel down." Palm muting is a very effective and widely used technique in metal music, creating a heavy, chunky feel while expanding the dramatic quality as well. If you are using a pick, make sure to use the palm of your hand to deaden the string somewhat as you strike it. If you are a fingerstyle player, you can use your left hand to help mute out the note by lightening up on the string just a bit.

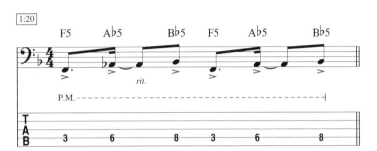

Words and Music by
James Hetfield, Lars Ulrich, Kirk Hammett and Bob Rock

Invisible Kid

OPENING RIFF

Note that this song utilizes a five-string bass tuned, low to high, G#–C#–G–C–F; however, this riff and the others in this song use only the two lowest strings. The opening riff has an extremely aggressive feel, utilizing all of the rhythmic tightness that is signature Metallica, played in the low range. The intensity of the galloping rhythms (the two 16th notes/one eighth note pattern) is undeniable. The trick here is to play the riff cleanly with the utmost concentration on accuracy, given the low range. For pick players, alternate picking may be the answer for pulling off this groove, while fingerstyle players should try to alternate between at least two fingers.

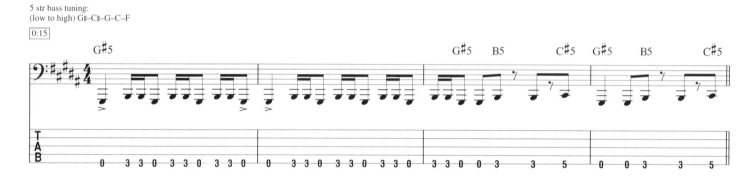

VERSE RIFF

The Verse riff has many of the same elements as the opening riff. The rhythm is scaled down a bit to accommodate the vocals and matches them in a number of spots. The G# pentatonic minor scale is the central force here. In the last measure of the phrase, the bass and guitars move in parallel motion with the bass, doubling two octaves below.

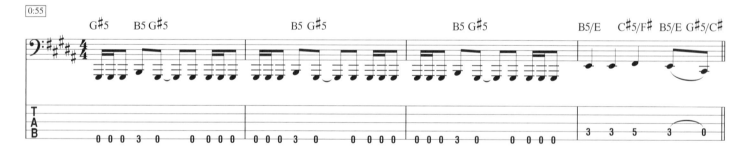

PRE-CHORUS/CHORUS RIFF

This riff is like a time bomb just waiting to explode under the haunting vocal line. While staying in the same key (G# minor), the riff basically ascends chromatically up to the B, a minor 3rd away. The chords change on the weak beats, which give an otherwise ordinary rhythmic pattern a syncopated feel. The last measure is slightly different to help distinguish the end of the phrase.

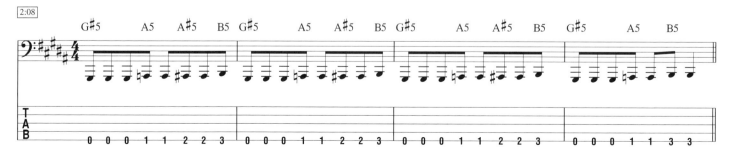

TAG RIFF

At the end of the second Chorus, there is a short section that has a different sort of sound. The riff is odd because there is no downbeat, so there is an empty space at the top of the groove. Be sure to feel the beginning of each measure and resist the temptation to play on beat one. The riff ends with an eighth note whole step bend from B to C♯. Make sure not to release the bend back down—you can do this by muting the string after the bend with your right hand. Because of the rest on the first eighth note, there is time to regroup.

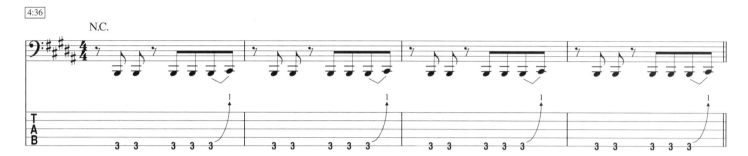

BRIDGE SECTION INTRO

The introduction to the Bridge section shows the groove taking a new turn, going from 4/4 to 3/4. Accents on the first beat along with the snare drum hits on beats 1 and 3 help to stabilize the feel. The tonality of the riff changes slightly with the use of A♮ in the last measure, giving off a darker sound. This is because of its half step relationship with the tonic, G♯.

Words and Music by
James Hetfield, Lars Ulrich, Kirk Hammett and Bob Rock

My World

VERSE RIFF

Note that this song utilizes a five-string bass in drop D tuning, down one whole step. The Verse riff stays steady with accented eighth notes before finishing by doubling the guitar riff. The groove is based on the minor pentatonic scale. The accents in measures 3 and 4 mirror the accents of the guitar part in the previous two measures. To really feel the effect of this and give good support, make sure to accent the eighth note Ds on beat 1, the "and" of beat 2, and beat 4.

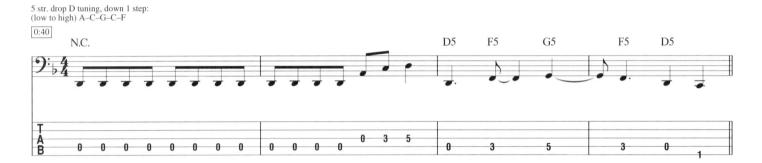

HALF TIME FEEL

The half time feel comes between Verses. The riff is mainly a rhythmic shadow of the drumbeat. . .

. . . which appears later in the song with a more syncopated line

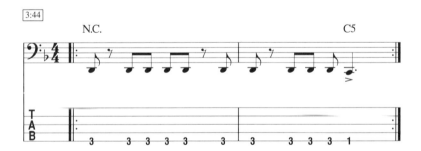

OUT OF THEIR HEADS

At the end of the Chorus, preceding the words "out of my head," Metallica shows that they can still stun with their expertly crafted riffs. This one is surprising because of its odd phrasing—it's over a measure of 4/4 with an added measure of 2/4. Based on the D blues scale, it starts out very syncopated, making use of the offbeats going between the D and F before finishing on the G and A♭.

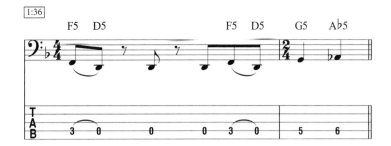

OUTRO RIFF

The Outro riff features Rock on the bass laying down a refreshing line based on the D blues scale. It's centered on the pedal point D while it travels up and down the blues scale, peaking on the "blue note," A♭. This is tricky to play at this speed, so be sure to coordinate—your left hand should lift off before you strike the open string. Accenting the moving line will help to bring it out to the forefront while also keeping your timing steady.

Words and Music by
James Hetfield, Lars Ulrich, Kirk Hammett and Bob Rock

Copyright © 2003 Creeping Death Music (ASCAP), EMI Blackwood (Canada) Music Ltd.
and Mahina Hoku Publishing
All Rights for EMI Blackwood (Canada) Music Ltd. and Mahina Hoku Publishing
Controlled and Administered by EMI Blackwood Music Inc.
International Copyright Secured   All Rights Reserved

Shoot Me Again

INTRO RIFF

Note that this song utilizes a five-string bass in drop D tuning, down one whole step. A highlight of the Intro riff is Rock's solid bass lick—an octave pattern with a half step neighbor tone (E♭). Played five times, the last iteration really stands out due to the soloing on the riff. Playing this can be a challenge because every note is articulated—practice at a slow tempo until you have it all in your fingers. In the second half of the riff, he takes it down an octave and changes the pattern, going more to the E♭ and using the Ds as accent spots following the accents of the rhythm guitars.

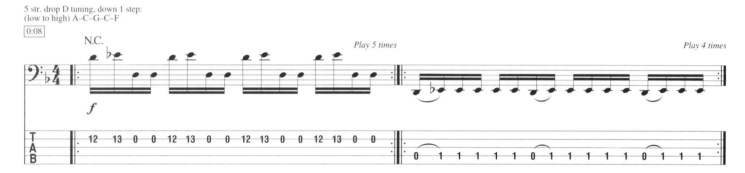

VERSE RIFF

The Verse riff is somewhat complex in that the timing can throw you off if you're not ready for it! It moves from a D5 up a half step two measures later to an E♭5 chord. Under these chords, the rhythmic patterns are tricky, mixing the beat up with 16th note/eighth note combinations. The third measure is the most difficult—maintain the rhythm pattern while adding the half step bend at the beginning.

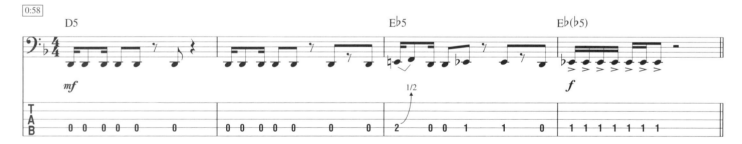

PRE-CHORUS RIFF

At the Verse, the bass is heard loud and clear in a variation with the low D. At the end of the first measure, an offbeat hammer-on followed by a muffled note provide some syncopated heaviness. The guitars enter in the second measure as the riff gets more chromatic, moving through the E♭ chord and finishing on the F.

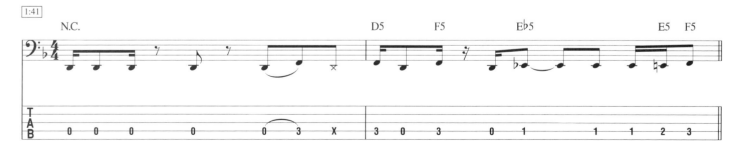

FLOATING RHYTHMS

In the Bridge section of the song, a "floating rhythm figure" appears. These are patterns that go through a cycle and have the feeling of floating through measures because the downbeat may sound "lost"—the feel isn't grounded until it comes back on the beat. The pattern here is two 16th notes followed by a 16th rest. Don't try to force the rhythm; just be steady and consistent. It will take its course and eventually fall back into place.

Words and Music by
James Hetfield, Lars Ulrich, Kirk Hammett and Bob Rock

Copyright © 2003 Creeping Death Music (ASCAP), EMI Blackwood (Canada) Music Ltd.
and Mahina Hoku Publishing
All Rights for EMI Blackwood (Canada) Music Ltd. and Mahina Hoku Publishing
Controlled and Administered by EMI Blackwood Music Inc.
International Copyright Secured   All Rights Reserved

Sweet Amber

DOUBLE TIME OPENING RIFF

Note that this song utilizes a five-string bass in drop D tuning, down one whole step. This killer riff locks in tight with the drums and guitar. It's a tricky groove to get in sync because of the speed and complexity of the rhythm. Start out slowly to understand the how the chords move. The whole step bend towards the end of the phrase takes some power to execute accurately, given that the F is played in the lower area of the neck and has to be bent to a G—two fingers can be used.

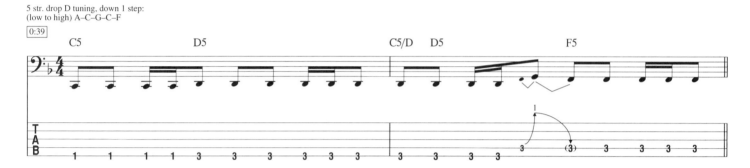

PRE-CHORUS RIFF

The C chord is anticipated into measure 3 with a short and quick eighth note. Measure 4 is a fantastic display of solid rhythm playing as the line follows the chord changes, going right along with the bass drum hits. This is a great example of smart rhythm section playing.

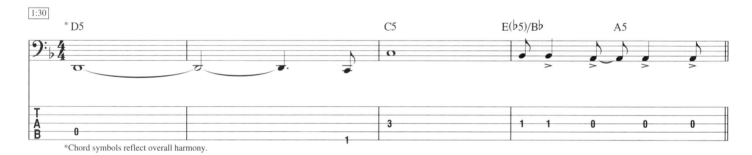

*Chord symbols reflect overall harmony.

The next part of the riff is a thick groove, jamming on low open Ds. In measures 2 and 4, take note of how the line, based in D minor, moves through the F5 on beat 2 and the E5 on beat 4.

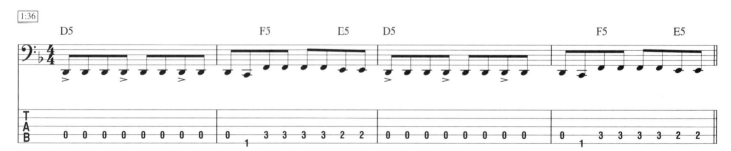

CHORUS RIFF

The 3/4 Chorus section is a cool and diverse part that has space in contrast to the jam-packed 4/4 sections. Try to feel each measure as one beat subdivided into three and you will understand the heaviness that this groove puts out. This is a D pentatonic minor progression going from D5 to the III chord (F5) and finishing on the iv chord (G5).

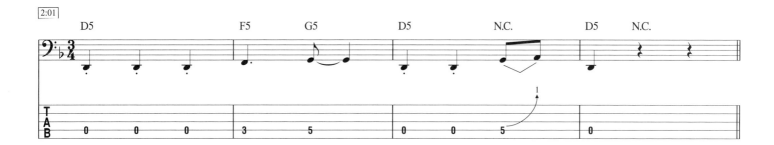

BASS LICK

Rock pulls off a great lick in the interlude before the second Verse. As Hetfield rips through the opening riff, Rock jumps out at you with a very distinctive slide to the upper octave D and, while holding there, plays the intense rhythm figure that is in the opening groove.

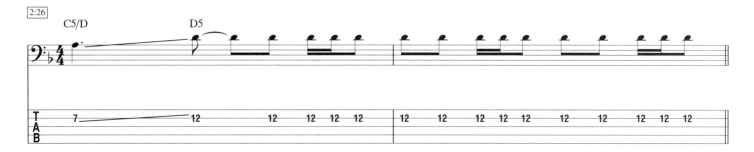

BRIDGE RIFF

The Bridge riff requires some agile right-hand work—there is speed picking galore, and it is just plain *fast*. Every other measure is marked with a transitional quarter note to set up the next chord—these are also a good opportunities to (quickly!) rest your right hand. The F and D quarter notes in measure 2 surround the bass of the upcoming Dsus2/E chord.

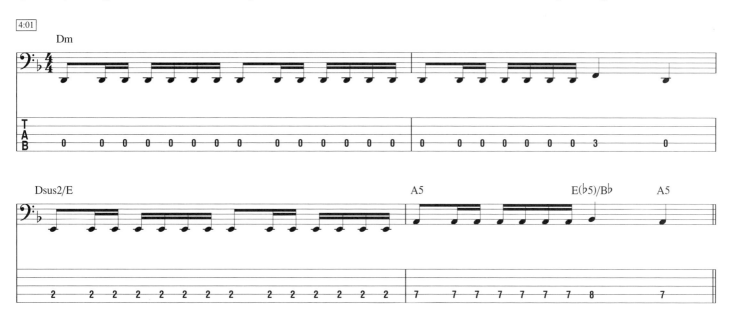

Words and Music by
ames Hetfield, Lars Ulrich, Kirk Hammett and Bob Rock

Copyright © 2003 Creeping Death Music (ASCAP), EMI Blackwood (Canada) Music Ltd.
and Mahina Hoku Publishing
All Rights for EMI Blackwood (Canada) Music Ltd. and Mahina Hoku Publishing
Controlled and Administered by EMI Blackwood Music Inc.
International Copyright Secured   All Rights Reserved

The Unnamed Feeling

FIRST INTRO RIFF

Note that this song utilizes a five-string bass in drop D tuning, down one whole step. Syncopation defines this riff, with scattered groupings of eighth notes throughout the four-measure phrase. It is a great contrasting rhythm against the steady drumbeat. This is definitely difficult to play under a vocal line because of the precision needed to put the notes in the right places. Feeling the quarter note pulse can help you to get this riff tight.

5 str. drop D tuning, down 1 step:
(low to high) A–C–G–C–F

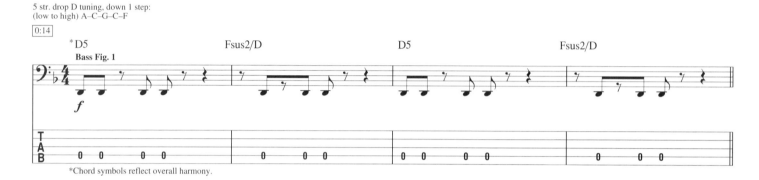

*Chord symbols reflect overall harmony.

SECOND INTRO RIFF

The bass here makes its presence known by nailing out a hip line full of bends. The line moves under the guitar rhythmic hits. On the second and fourth beats, Rock quickly bends up a half step from the E to the F, releasing on the second eighth note back down to the E.

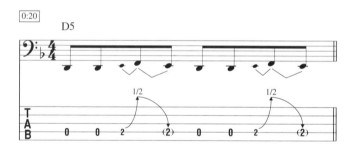

A variation of this riff occurs later in the song with a combination of 3/4 and 5/4 meters. The bends occur more frequently in this version.

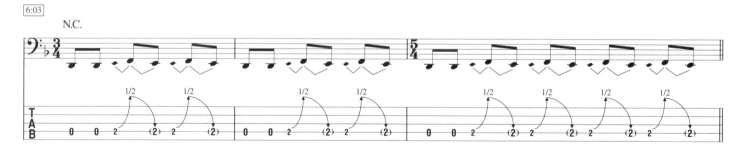

CHORUS RIFF (FIRST TIME)

The Chorus riff starts out with hits that mirror the bass drum, and there is a definite method to this madness. In several places, an eighth note anticipation of each upcoming chord marks the end of each measure, while a C acts as a sort of common tone, regardless of the chord. This is a creative melodic technique, coupled with rhythmic hits, that is both subtle and effective.

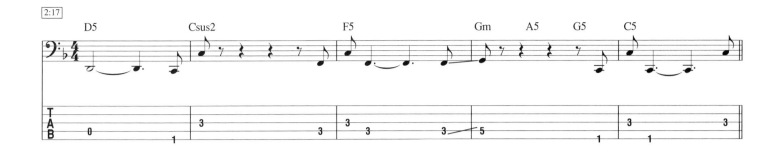

CHORUS RIFF (SECOND TIME)

The rhythm takes precedence in the second Chorus riff. Harmonically, it is straightforward, going in between D5 and C5 chords and adding in F5 and G5. Measure 3 acts as a rhythmic answer to measure 1. This section interacts well against the vocal line and acts almost like another voice of dialogue. Things get more rhythmically aggressive as they progress.

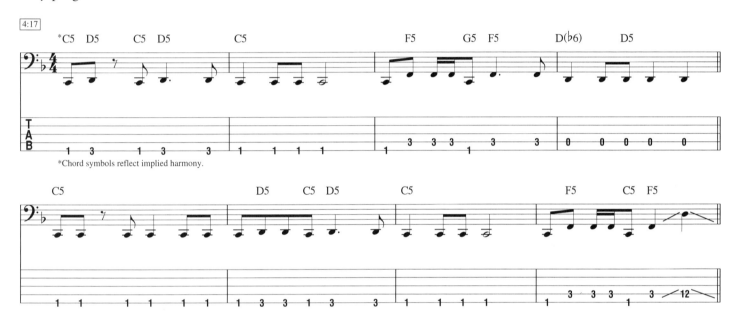

*Chord symbols reflect implied harmony.

INTERLUDE SECTION

The Interlude features the rhythmic syncopation of the Verse riff. As the riff moves on, the note D acts as a pedal point for the increasingly moving chords to climatic effect.

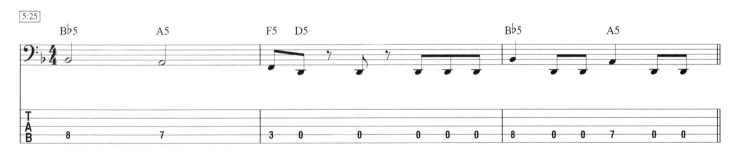

Words and Music by
James Hetfield, Lars Ulrich, Kirk Hammett and Bob Rock

Purify

FIRST INTRO RIFF

Note that this song utilizes a five-string bass in drop D tuning, down one whole step. Getting the feel of this riff makes for a challenge—it has tied and hammered-on notes in crucial parts of the measures, which can come fast at this type of tempo. Play the riff slowly at first and take out the slurs and ties; this will enable you to hear and feel how the notes move in rhythm. When you feel comfortable with the timing, increase the tempo and add back the ties and hammer-ons.

5str. drop D tuning, down 1 step:
(low to high) A–C–G–C–F

The first measure of this riff returns later in the song—note that the tie has been removed.

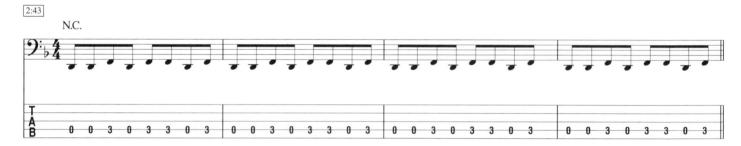

SECOND INTRO RIFF

The Verse riff follows the guitars' chromatically pushed groove. Eighth notes plow through the first two chords, while quarter notes mark the A5 and D5 chords.

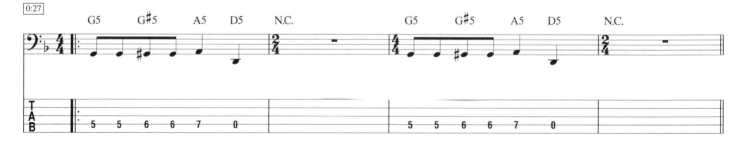

The empty 2/4 measures in the Intro section get filled in with a cool connecting line in the version that appears in the second half of the Verse.

CHORUS RIFF

In the second half of the Chorus, Rock doubles the guitars with another heavy groove. This riff also has similarities to the second Intro riff in its shape with its ascending chromatic opening, but moves through the notes at twice the speed, all around the key of D minor.

BRIDGE RIFF

The Bridge moves through a series of chords laid out in tight formation. After the A, the chords move in 5ths starting from the Fsus2. The rhythm sticks closely to that of the drums. Keep the notes short—a challenge within such a fast moving tempo.

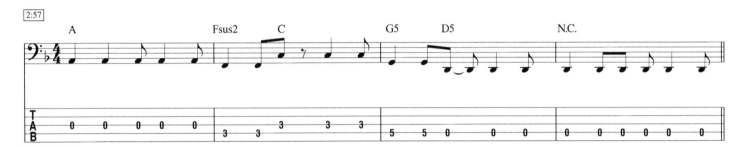

Words and Music by
James Hetfield, Lars Ulrich, Kirk Hammett and Bob Rock

Copyright © 2003 Creeping Death Music (ASCAP), EMI Blackwood (Canada) Music Ltd.
and Mahina Hoku Publishing
All Rights for EMI Blackwood (Canada) Music Ltd. and Mahina Hoku Publishing
Controlled and Administered by EMI Blackwood Music Inc.
International Copyright Secured   All Rights Reserved

All Within My Hands

This song features great examples of riff development with themes and variations.

INTRO RIFF

Note that this song utilizes a five-string bass in drop D tuning, down one whole step. This is a good example of the floating rhythm concept also seen in "Shoot Me Again." Here, we have a pattern of two eighth notes with an eighth note rest that repeats over two measures, finishing with a long F. When getting into the feel of a "fast 4," be prepared to play on the weak parts of beats as well as the strong parts.

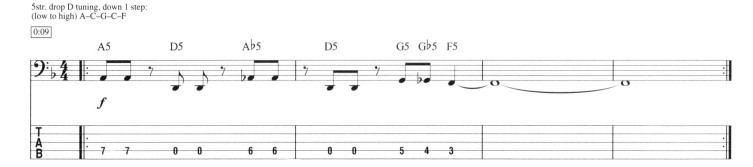

The Intro riff is brought back in many different forms. Here's a variation that occurs immediately after the first example. In this variation, the eighth note rests are "filled in," giving the groove a more legato feel.

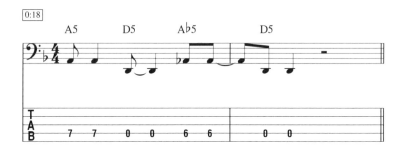

The variation that appears in the Chorus is a combination of the Intro riff and the first variation. It's notated differently because of the half time feel, but it is essentially the same riff.

INTERLUDE RIFF

The Interlude riff is a chromatic groove based on the D blues scale. The melodic pattern changes in the second measure—the line moves from F through to G before settling on the low D. Use a 1–2–3 left-hand fingering approach over the chromatic line to ensure a smooth execution. In the second measure, make sure to shift your position on the neck while keeping the same fingering.

SECOND INTERLUDE RIFF

In the second Interlude after the Verse, a variation of the previous riff comes into play. Notice the tied notes over the second beat and over the barline. This shifts the rhythm a bit before finishing with a bluesy lick—a half step bend from the G to the "blue note" A♭ that is then released down the scale. Play this with two fingers: one for the bend and one for the resolution (F). This riff goes on to define the Chorus section.

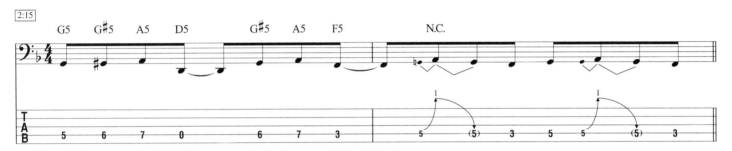

A combination of the two Interlude riffs happens later in the song, just before the Bridge section. The chromatic line is retained in the first measure, and the bluesy bend is shifted to the second measure.

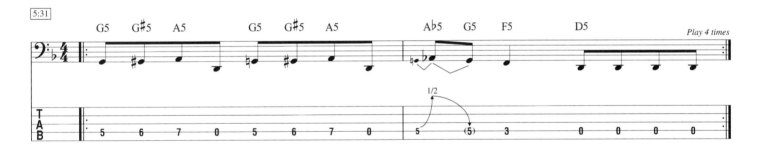

THIRD INTERLUDE RIFF

This is yet another Interlude variation.

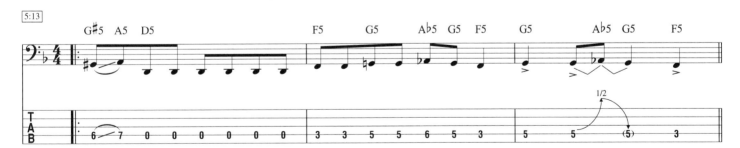

Bass Notation Legend

Bass music can be notated two different ways: on a *musical staff*, and in *tablature*.

THE MUSICAL STAFF shows pitches and rhythms and is divided by bar lines into measures. Pitches are named after the first seven letters of the alphabet.

TABLATURE graphically represents the bass fingerboard. Each horizontal line represents a string, and each number represents a fret.

3rd string, open   2nd string, 2nd fret   1st & 2nd strings open, played together

HAMMER-ON: Strike the first (lower) note with one finger, then sound the higher note (on the same string) with another finger by fretting it without picking.

PULL-OFF: Place both fingers on the notes to be sounded. Strike the first note and without picking, pull the finger off to sound the second (lower) note.

LEGATO SLIDE: Strike the first note and then slide the same fret-hand finger up or down to the second note. The second note is not struck.

SHIFT SLIDE: Same as legato slide, except the second note is struck.

TRILL: Very rapidly alternate between the notes indicated by continuously hammering on and pulling off.

TREMOLO PICKING: The note is picked as rapidly and continuously as possible.

VIBRATO: The string is vibrated by rapidly bending and releasing the note with the fretting hand.

SHAKE: Using one finger, rapidly alternate between two notes on one string by sliding either a half-step above or below.

NATURAL HARMONIC: Strike the note while the fret hand lightly touches the string directly over the fret indicated.

MUFFLED STRINGS: A percussive sound is produced by laying the fret hand across the string(s) without depressing them and striking them with the pick hand.

BEND: Strike the note and bend up the interval shown.

BEND AND RELEASE: Strike the note and bend up as indicated, then release back to the original note. Only the first note is struck.

RIGHT-HAND TAP: Hammer ("tap") the fret indicated with the "pick-hand" index or middle finger and pull off to the note fretted by the fret hand.

LEFT-HAND TAP: Hammer ("tap") the fret indicated with the "fret-hand" index or middle finger.

SLAP: Strike ("slap") string with right-hand thumb.

POP: Snap ("pop") string with right-hand index or middle finger.

Additional Musical Definitions

 (accent) • Accentuate note (play it louder)

 (accent) • Accentuate note with great intensity

 (staccato) • Play the note short

⊓ • Downstroke

∨ • Upstroke

D.S. al Coda • Go back to the sign (𝄋), then play until the measure marked "***To Coda***," then skip to the section labelled "**Coda**."

D.C. al Fine • Go back to the beginning of the song and play until the measure marked "***Fine***" (end).

Bass Fig. • Label used to recall a recurring pattern.

Fill • Label used to identify a brief pattern which is to be inserted into the arrangement.

tacet • Instrument is silent (drops out).

 • Repeat measures between signs.

 • When a repeated section has different endings, play the first ending only the first time and the second ending only the second time.

NOTE: Tablature numbers in parentheses mean:
1. The note is being sustained over a system (note in standard notation is tied), or
2. The note is sustained, but a new articulation (such as a hammer-on, pull-off, slide or vibrato begins), or
3. The note is a barely audible "ghost" note (note in standard notation is also in parentheses).